Praise for *Out of Place in Time and Space*

"A marvelously quirky, intensely interesting, and engagingly written romp that will fascinate, entertain, and, above all, make you think! Wood reveals some truly remarkable 'out of place' marvels that run the gamut from computers to concrete, submarines to flying saucers, 'death rays' to 'disappearing' planets. He makes you question what you thought you knew about history."

—Jerry D. Morelock, PhD, editor in chief,
Armchair General magazine

"Lamont Wood's *Out of Place in Time and Space* is surprising, fascinating, and delightful. He has assembled amazing tales of prescience—people who saw far ahead and were frequently ignored—and he tells these stories crisply and well, with no frills."

—Ted Nelson, futurist, inventor of hypertext

"The Internet was invented in 1945. The ancient Greeks almost perfected the death ray. England's King Henry V underwent antiseptic facial surgery more than 400 years before such surgery was supposedly invented. And Lamont Wood's book describing all this, and more, was published in 2011. Reverse anachronism or mere coincidence? You decide."

—Peter Krass, founder and president of Petros Consulting

Out of Place in Time and Space

Inventions, Beliefs, and Artistic Anomalies That
Were Impossibly Ahead of Their Time

By Lamont Wood

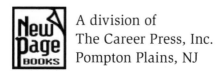

A division of
The Career Press, Inc.
Pompton Plains, NJ

OUT OF PLACE IN TIME AND SPACE
EDITED BY KATHRYN HENCHES
TYPESET BY DIANA GHAZZAWI
Cover design by Ian Shimkoviak/the BookDesigners
Printed in the U.S.A.

To order this title, please call toll-free 1-800-CAREER-1 (NJ and Canada: 201-848-0310) to order using VISA or MasterCard, or for further information on books from Career Press.

The Career Press, Inc.
220 West Parkway, Unit 12
Pompton Plains, NJ 07444
www.careerpress.com
www.newpagebooks.com

Library of Congress Cataloging-in-Publication Data
Wood, Lamont, 1953-
    Out of place in time and space : inventions, beliefs, and artistic anomalies that were impossibly ahead of their time / by Lamont Wood.
        p. cm.
    Includes bibliographical references and index.
    ISBN 978-1-60163-178-7 – ISBN 978-1-60163-648-5 (ebook) 1. Curiosities and wonders. 2. History--Miscellanea. I. Title.

AG243.W5895 2011
031'.02--dc23
                                                2011016115

Acknowledgments

I would like to thank my wife, Dr. Louise O'Donnell, psychologist, and professor at the University of Texas Health Science Center at San Antonio, for putting up with my service to this book. Meanwhile, my agent, Jeff Herman, seemed to understand what I was doing better than I did—but maybe that's what agents are for. The staff at New Page Books were also refreshingly decisive. I would also like to thank Keith Ferrell, former editor of *OMNI* magazine, for his encouragement, and for his help with the publicity material.

Contents

Preface

This book wrote itself. Doubtless you've encountered such statements before and rightly dismissed them as claptrap, but in this case there is a certain degree of truth to it. While pondering certain examples of events that seemed to defy the commonly accepted rules of time and causality, the idea for the book came to me fully formed, demanding that I write it. It was as if it already existed and that by working on it I was merely performing some sort of liturgy in its honor. But considering the subject matter, that seemed only natural.

Even so, I might have dismissed the urge, except that I was attending the Asilomar Microcomputer Conference in California and mentioned the "Madonna and Child With Toy Helicopter" to the person on my left during a cafeteria-style lunch. She turned out to be Dr. Suzanne M. Fischer, associate curator of technology at the Henry Ford Museum in Dearborn, Michigan. I expressed mystification about how to find the painting, knowing only that it was in a European museum. As soon as she got back to her office the next week she used her expertise to find it, sending me background material about it.

So I was not even the first person to serve the book's ends. Apparently it has a life of its own—although, admittedly, that life is ultimately derived from the work that I put into it, and the hours it stole from my family. I can only hope that the results that you are holding justify it.

Introduction

Of course, the moons of Mars could not have been described 151 years before they were discovered, or the Apollo Program a century before it took place, or the Pacific War 16 years before it started. An ancient Roman army could not have been defeated by huge machines. A medieval painting could not have depicted a flying toy helicopter. The world's best preserved ancient building cannot lack an obvious purpose, and cannot have been built with modern methods.

Guess again.

That such things cannot exist, at least not according to commonly accepted historical timelines, not to mention mainstream theories of the nature of time and causality, is beyond dispute. Yet, their existence is also beyond dispute. Actually, such phenomena appear to be plentiful—hiding in plain sight, so to speak.

In fact, not only do they turn out to be plentiful, but they often turn out to have features in common, so that they lend themselves to classification, just like microorganisms or astronomical bodies.

First and least controversial are the bleeding-edge phenomena, which are usually associated with the latest technology or ideas. Bleeding-edge phenomena are those that take place far enough ahead of the leading-edge wave that the participants really don't know what they're doing, and suffer for it. Someone building a submarine in 1900 was on the leading edge. Someone building a submarine in 1863 (and drowning in it) was on the bleeding edge.

Next come the anachronisms. With bleeding edge phenomena you can usually estimate how premature the perpetrators were, but with anachronisms about all you can say is that the thing in question is completely out of place, time-wise. Meanwhile, it appears that there are two kinds of anachronisms, conventional and reverse. We might also call them non-threatening, and disturbing.

The conventional anachronisms are the non-threatening variety, in which objects from the present show up in fictional depictions of the past (such as people wearing wristwatches in movies about Rome) or the future (such as lady starship crew members in the original *Star Trek* TV series wearing miniskirts and makeup from the 1960s).

But reverse anachronisms do not involve fictional depictions, but actual objects, practices, or information—and that's why they're disturbing. Whereas conventional anachronisms are an annoyance for attentive movie audiences, reverse anachronisms are an indication that the space-time continuum might be a little porous in spots. (Or that someone needs to do some big-time explaining—read on and judge the results for yourself.)

This book ignores conventional anachronisms and focuses on reverse anachronisms. You'd think they'd be quite rare, but in fact they keep popping up. At least two kinds of reverse anachronisms can be identified:

- The first kind involves objects, beliefs, or practices from our present that show up in the past.
- The second kind involves objects, beliefs, or practices from our future that show up in the past.

You could also make a case for reverse anachronisms of the third kind, involving objects, beliefs, or practices from our present that were, in the past, depicted in a future setting, as in 19th-century science fiction describing what is now the present. But let's not get carried away.

Most of the examples in this book are reverse anachronisms of the first kind. They leap out at us because they appear to belong to our present (or near past). They would appear to be impossible—but there they are.

But if reverse anachronisms of the first kind are impossible, those of the second kind would seem to be inconceivable—how would we recognize something from the future? Basically, we can't—but we can acknowledge that we can't figure something out, opening the door to the possibility of it being from the future.

But before you dismiss the previous sentence as new-age mumbo-jumbo, consider this: Many of the examples in this book actually started out as reverse anachronisms of the second kind (that is, from the future). Then time passed and they came into harmony with their settings. Beholders then appreciated them for what they were. Suddenly, they were reverse anachronisms of the first kind.

A classic example is the Antikythera Mechanism. When this corroded jumble of gears was found on the Greek seabed in 1901 it was accepted as a clockwork mystery. Throughout the next century, as computers came into daily use, it was seen for what it was—an ancient computer. So it shifted from a reverse anachronism of the second kind to one of the first kind.

Frankly, we may be surrounded at all times by reverse anachronisms of the second kind, but we are not equipped to recognize them. Other possible candidates in the book include the Voynich Manuscript, or the astronomical phenomena. At some point they may come into synch with the present, and we will be able to fully appreciate them. Until then we can only confront them with our logic, whose adequacy the reader is invited to judge.

Beyond the bleeding edge and the anachronisms there is, basically, noise. Of course, noise is unintelligible input that you end up ignoring—but you can hear voices in it if you listen hard enough. Likewise, there are examples in this book of material that initially seems out of place in the space-time continuum, and may have followers that embrace them as such. (The flying saucers found in Renaissance church art are an example.) But logic indicates that they are out of place only in the minds of their followers, who inserted their own meaning in place of input that made no sense to them. But there is a fully convincing and fully mundane explanation for each one—an explanation that does not challenge the concept of time or causality.

Unless, of course, the examples turn out to be reverse anachronisms of the second kind, and we only think that we understand what we are looking at. We can't rule out that possibility until the end of time arrives. In the meantime we have to rely on our logic to guide us.

But now that we've introduced the concept of logic and explanations, it's time to confront the central question: Is there some reassuring, cosmic explanation for the potentially disturbing phenomena described in this book?

Short answer: no, but read the book.

Middling answer: The typical example has its own explanation, which will probably be convincing mostly to those predisposed to be convinced. Read the book and you'll see.

Long answer: Queue up some ominous background music and imagine a bearded, avuncular man in a tweed sweater fixing you with his stare and saying, "There are more things in heaven and earth than are included in your philosophy." ("Philosophy" was a synonym for "science" in the days when avuncular men wore tweed.) You tartly reply, "That's a given!" Then turn off the imaginary music and read the book.

Meanwhile, if you were scanning ahead for mentions of UFOs, Atlantis, or ancient astronauts, then here is where your eyes will have come to rest. In answer to your unspoken question, no, the book does not invoke UFOs, ancient astronauts, or our busy friends from Atlantis as an explanation. Admittedly, that would be a lot more fun than undertaking the research that would point to rational explanations—especially when the rational explanations sometimes turn out to be pretty weak. Anyway, there is no conclusive proof that ancient astronauts, touring UFOs, or Atlanteans were not involved. And there never will be such proof, because you can't prove a negative. But do read the book—the author will not be offended by second-guessing. (See Chapter 8.)

If you were scanning for mentions of time travel, here is where your eyes will have come to rest. Time travel is a rational explanation on the assumption that it will eventually be invented. (Of course, UFOs, Atlanteans, and ancient astronauts become rational explanations if they, too, are scientifically confirmed.) As will be noted throughout the book, some of the phenomena beg for a time-traveler explanation. With others, however, someone from the future, with actual foreknowledge, would surely have behaved in an entirely different manner. Read the book and you'll see. (Of course, that assumes that time travelers from the far future think like we do. They might have their own agendas.)

Finally, if you were scanning ahead for mentions of "Occam's Razor" or "rational explanations," then you've come to the right place. Unfortunately, there's little to say on these topics—there is no blanket explanation for reverse anachronisms or any other form of out-of-placeness. Unless, of course, it seems fair to say that the past is prologue to the present, and that the present is prologue to the future—which some people started writing in the past. In other words, we may have to at least consider the possibility that people in the past were as clever as we are, albeit not always as well-informed by the cumulative results of organized, well-funded, peer-reviewed, Internet-circulated science.

And that stuff happens, irrespective of organized, well-funded, peer-reviewed, Internet-circulated science. Read on.

MACHINES: PHYSICAL OR DESCRIBED

Of course, all technology derives from some previous technology. For instance, ocean liners were developed from smaller ships that were developed from ocean-going canoes, which were developed from dug-out canoes, and so on. Industrial steam engines were developed from low-pressure steam engines, which were developed from air-pressure steam engines...airplanes were developed from gliders, and so on.

Wrong.

Basically, the lead paragraph makes for satisfying stories, well worth telling over a campfire to young people who need to be assured that the world beyond the flickering light does make sense. But they're myths—they break down when you hit the "etc."

The only water transport cruder than a dug-out canoe is a man swimming with a plank as a life buoy, and there is no obvious way to derive a canoe from what that man is doing. The only thing cruder than an air-pressure (Newcomen) steam engine is a boiling pot on a stove, and no one ever used that to produce mechanical power. The only thing cruder than a glider is someone with feathers glued to his arms jumping off a cliff, and that led to nothing but injury.

In other words, you can't keep simplifying a device or removing components from it and think you're tracing its development, back to the point where the first atoms came together after the Big Bang. Technology and human ingenuity does not work that way.

Instead, at some point someone had to invent something new and useful. After that, development proceeded as people who used it found ways to make improvements.

This section is devoted to evidence of people inventing something new and potentially useful, in ways that defy modern conceptions or timelines of technological development. Typically it happened long before anyone else was prepared to appreciate what they were doing, and their innovation was abandoned.

Of course, it's a shame that they were not appreciated, and that their efforts ultimately could not overcome the mental rigidity of their times. But, that said, the point is not the marvel at the stupidity of our forebears (except maybe around the campfire.) Rather, we should examine our own mental rigidity. Right now, someone is inventing, from nothing, something that could start the next technological revolution. Will they be appreciated?

Read on, and judge the likelihood for yourself.

1
Virgin and Child With Toy Helicopter

Detail of a 1460 painting in which the Christ child is depicted as playing with a toy helicopter more than three centuries before its documented invention. Virgin and Child With St. Benedict, *from the Priory of St. Hippolytus of Vivoin (oil on panel) by the 15th-century French School, in the Musee de Tesse, Le Mans, France, through the Bridgeman Art Library. Used with permission.*

Progress, like the march of time, moves in definable, obvious steps. In terms of the development of the helicopter, we can see a clear progression from the first flying model in 1784 to the first man-carrying hop in 1906 to a fully functional machine in 1936 and full-scale production less than a decade later.

And if you accept the previous paragraph without reservation then you're going to have trouble with the *Virgin and Child With St Benedict*, one panel of a triptych that was painted about 1460. It is credited to the Master of Vivoin, otherwise known as an "unknown local artist," and is now in the Musee de Tesse in Le Mans, France.

You'll note that the Christ child is depicted as playing with a pull-string toy helicopter. As reconstructed, the string he is pulling is wrapped around a rod that is hanging within the hollow handle. Affixed to the top of the rod are four appropriately angled rotor blades. Pulling the string will spin the rod-rotor assembly, causing it to shoot into the air. This, you'll note, was more than three centuries before the first historically accepted working helicopter model was built.

Yes, Leonardo da Vinci did famously conceptualize the helicopter. However, he was 8 years old when this painting was made, and the device he designed, like the toy in the painting, had no mechanism for dampening torque. The rotor at the end of the tail boom in most helicopters serves that purpose. Without such a mechanism the body of the craft will spin in the opposite direction as the rotor (albeit slower because it weighs more), making it impractical for manned flight.

These days, helicopters have become part of the environment. Any toy similar to the one pictured would be seen as a toy helicopter. The toy flying rotors that the author has seen were actually simpler, and required the user to spin the rod with a hand-wipe motion.

But in a world where helicopters (or any other flying machine) did not exist, how was such a toy conceived? Anyone taking a jaunt in the time machine back to the 15th century bearing the gift of flight would surely have imparted information about air foils and gliders, which would actually be simpler and would lend themselves better to manned flight.

Meanwhile, watching clouds and birds inspired dreamers to invent balloons and airplanes. But the only natural analogy to the helicopter is the sycamore seed, which autogiros from the tree to the ground. Watching such seeds would probably inspire only vertigo.

The simplest explanation is that the toy evolved from a powered whirligig. A whirligig is a toy with colored rotors that spin in the wind (or when you wave it), producing a kaleidoscope of color and possibly some noise. The depiction of a whirligig allowed the artist to introduce a Christian cross motif into a composition, and so whirligigs occasionally show up in Christ child paintings.

At some point someone must have discovered that, in the absence of wind, you can power the whirligig by hand, and if it gets away from you the results can be very entertaining, especially to a small boy. Some sources trace this toy to ancient China, although the evidence seems slight. However, if it arose there and then, it presumably evolved the same way, as a powered whirligig.

And so the toy helicopter became humanity's first flying machine. Yet, it appears to have had no impact on the progress of technology. Its potential was ignored for centuries. Doubtless it was dismissed as a toy, too frivolous for serious study.

But of course it was also clearly a reverse anachronism of the second kind, an object that could not be appreciated in its day because it was from a future setting. With helicopters being part of our present, we can appreciate it as a reverse anachronism of the first kind.

Wheeled toys have been found in Incan tombs, yet the Incans did not use wheeled transportation on their extensive system of paved roads. It makes you wonder about what kids are playing with these days, and if we should pay closer attention. For instance, if we understood the complex dynamics of the cup-and-ball, would it lead to some culture-altering breakthrough? And then there's that thing they chant while playing rope: "...ashes, ashes, we all fall down!"

On second thought, maybe ignorance is bliss.

2
The Ancient Computer

A large fragment of the Antikythera Mechanism, a corroded mass of gears found on the Greek seabed in 1901, and now understood to be a Roman-era computer. Wikimedia Commons image by Marsyas. Used under license.

The development of elaborate but precise gear chains is associated with the making of clocks, crude examples of which started appearing in Europe in about 1300. Development was continuous, with reasonable accuracy (meaning the loss of only a minute per day) attained by about 1600. Chronometers that could support accurate oceanic navigation started appearing after 1761. As far as complex geared calculating devices go, the first successful one was apparently built by Blaise Pascal in 1642. Especially complex epicyclic (otherwise known as planetary) gearing, with gears turning on axels that are themselves revolving around a gear, are not seen much until the rise of rotary machinery during the Industrial Revolution, when they were found handy for differentials.

Yes, the history of gears, clocks, and mechanical calculators meshes nicely (pun intended) as part of the bigger picture of time and linear progress marching smoothly from the past to the present.

Unfortunately, the existence of the Antikythera Mechanism throws a wrench into the intricate workings of that story, because it is a clock-like calculating device made from complex gearing—including epicyclic gears—that was made no later than 65 BC. Despite its modern patina, Julius Caesar could have consulted it.

The device was part of a trove of objects recovered from the Mediterranean seabed in 1901–1902 after sponge divers found a Roman wreck off Antikythera, a small island about 10 miles south-southeast of the larger island of Kythera (hence the name) in the strait between Greece and Crete. At first it appeared to be an encrusted block about the size of a large book—until it broke open, revealing a mass of corroded bronze gears. The mass turned out to be the largest fragment of the larger, original object, whatever it was, and in the end about 80 fragments were assigned to it. It's probable that more remain on the seabed.

It was obviously some kind of clockwork machine, but researches couldn't say much more about it than that, because it was badly damaged and the remaining parts were hopelessly cemented together. Advances in X-ray technology have since allowed researchers to literally probe inside the mass, precisely counting how many teeth there were on individual gears, and even reading text on components that are buried under other components. Meanwhile, computers have since become common currency—and aided the analysis of the mechanism.

The result of the work is a consensus that the Antikythera Mechanism (as it's been named) was a computer.

No, really—keep reading.

Cutting through the hype, we need to establish that it was not a computer in the sense that it could run software to figure the imperial budget, or help a scrivener compose papyrus scrolls. It's what they call an analog computer, meaning its mechanism is designed to mimic, in an "analogous" fashion, some physical phenomena in a way that lets the user predict or control some other phenomena. There was a time when all computers were analog computers. Models of the solar system with accurate ratios of planetary movement, controls for the Panama Canal, slide rules, geared systems formerly used to solve differential equations by integration, and old-style artillery fire control systems are examples of analog computers. Their programming is built into their designs, and they cannot be readily reprogrammed for some other task.

The upshot if that if it is truly an analog computer, analysis of the gears of the Antikythera Mechanism ought to reveal its purpose, assuming that enough remains of it to reveal anything. And after more than a century of work, the functions of 29 of its 30 surviving gears have been accounted for. (The holdout probably linked to components that remain on the seabed.)

The latest thought is that the object was a thick rectangular box with dials on the front and back, and an input crank on the side.

On one side were two large dials, each in the center of a spiral track. Both dials could extend with a slider so that their indicators could follow the track that wound around them, sliding along the track as it spiraled outward. One dial-and-spiral was for the Metonic cycle, and the other for the Saros cycle.

The Metonic cycle is a recurring cycle of resonance between the lunar and solar calendars, and can be used to reconcile the two calendars. This is necessary because using months based on lunar phases, and using months based on 12 divisions of the solar year, produce different results. However, both calendar styles were used then, and are still used today. The cycle covers 19 years or 235 lunar months.

The Saros cycle is a recurring pattern of lunar and solar eclipses that covers 223 months. It can be used to accurately predict both lunar and solar eclipses, but not all the solar eclipses will be visible at any one point on the globe.

There were also smaller dials on that side showing whether the date in question was during a year when the Olympics (or one of several other games) were held.

The other side had a large dial with multiple pointers. One was for setting or showing the date, and others indicated the resulting position of the sun and the moon in the zodiac, and one showed the lunar phases. There may have been another, now lost set of dials indicating the positions of the planets (which would have meant Mercury, Venus, Mars, Jupiter, and Saturn) but those components did not make it to the surface.

Presumably, the user could set a date and see what events and positions coincided, or set the events and positions and then check to see what date was involved. Or you could set a date and then crank the handle to simulate the passage of time and see what happened next. It would probably have been used in civic planning, to set the dates of holidays and festivals that were geared to astronomical events. (Easter is a modern example.) It would not have been useful for navigation.

Machines with this level of complexity would not be seen for another 1,500 years. On top of that, the gear train for the lunar movements is faithful to the fact that the moon's orbital speed increases as it gets closer to the Earth and slows down as it gets farther from the Earth (although the ancient astronomers would not have understood the phenomenon in those terms). To mimic these changing ratios, the designers used two sets of epicyclic (also called planetary) gears. Such gear trains would not be seen again until the Industrial Revolution. There's probably one in your car, assuming it has an automatic transmission.

Where did the device come from? Assuming some time traveler didn't get careless, we can assume it was a product of ancient Greek culture, because the text inscribed on it is Greek, and because it was found in Greek waters. The Roman warlord Sulla sacked Athens in 86 BC as part of the Roman Empire's effort to bring the Greeks to heel, and it's known that one of his shiploads of loot came to grief at Antikythera, which lies on the direct sea route from Athens to Rome. But analysis of the rest of the cargo that was found with the Antikythera Mechanism does not point to Athens as a point of origin, but some place farther east, such as Pergamon (in modern Turkey).

Whatever its port of embarkation, the text on the Antikythera Mechanism includes the names of months that were used in Corinth rather than Athens, indicating it was built (or intended for use) in that Greek city-state southwest of Athens, or in some colony of Corinth that shared its dialect. Corinth itself was sacked by the Romans in 146 BC and so is probably not a candidate for the machine's place of origin. Syracuse, the leading Greek city-state in Sicily, was a Corinthian colony. When it was sacked by the Romans (who did a lot of that) in 212 BC their commander is recorded as personally retaining only two pieces of loot, both being mechanical models demonstrating the movements of the solar system, made by Syracuse's most famous citizen, Archimedes. The general donated one to a Roman temple and the other became a family heirloom.

The Roman orator Cicero mentioned the heirloom version in one of his philosophical dialogues (written about 51 BC) that involved a descendent of the general. Cicero admitted that the whole thing was over his head, but on the other hand he didn't think that the device looked very impressive. Of course, the Antikythera Mechanism was outwardly just a box with dials and a crank. (Cicero also mentioned another, similar device made in his lifetime by an astronomer on Rhodes.)

Does this make the Antikythera Mechanism another footprint in the sands of time by the mad scientist of ancient Syracuse? We already have him making headlines for reverse-anachronistic war machines, death rays, calculus, and set theory (see Chapter 3) But, frankly, Archimedes died about a century and a half before the Antikythera Mechanism took the plunge (which the latest research indicates was in about 65 BC), so giving him direct credit seems like a stretch.

More likely, the machine was part of a tradition of geared scientific devices that stretched back to at least Archimedes. That some tinsmith decided to toss one together just before the ship sailed is inconceivable—its sophistication speaks to generations of development, not only in the design and machining of precise gears, but also in the faithful representation of astronomical movements. (And Cicero—no astronomer himself—offhand knew of three other such devices.)

A better question is how such skill could have evaporated. Presumably, times changed and information that such machines gave access to was no longer valued. The tradition of innovation that must have produced them was no longer valued, either. We can probably thank the Romans.

Meanwhile, the Antikythera Mechanism turns out to be a classic example of a reverse anachronism of the second kind, meaning that when it was first encountered it represented something from the beholder's future and therefore defied comprehension. Being a computer, it could not be understood in pre-computer 1901. Times have since caught up with it, turning it into a reverse anachronism of the first kind, as we ponder how this computer showed up in the past.

Of course, that assumes there is not something about it that we still have not discovered, something that would again make it a reverse anachronism of the second kind. There are still gears missing, after all.

3
Romans Versus the Machines

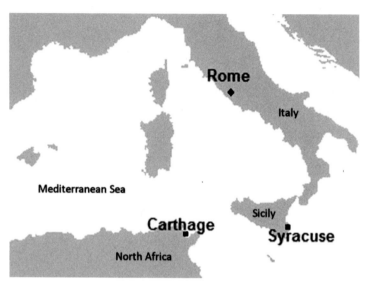

Syracuse's location in the central Mediterranean, showing its strategic position in the Rome-Carthage showdown. Map by the author.

The accounts of the siege of Syracuse in 214 BC read like an ancient "War of the Worlds." Mysterious giant machines rose up and smashed an assaulting Roman force. Only Roman discipline kept the attackers from collapsing in terror.

All in all, it comes off as cracking good science fiction in the best pulp novel tradition. If they made a movie out of *The Day the Earth Stood Still*, surely they'll get around to this story.

Unfortunately, the story is from ancient texts that have always been accepted as serious history. The episode was part of the heavily documented Punic Wars, the titanic death struggle between the Roman and Carthaginian empires that eventually involved most of the Mediterranean basin.

Syracuse was the leading city-state in Sicily and had been kept in the Roman camp by its ruling warlord for 55 prosperous, peaceful years. He also entrusted municipal defense planning to his younger kinsman, the mathematician Archimedes, son of Phidias. Archimedes evidently had all the time and resources needed to reshape the defenses of the city along engineering principles. Either he was secretive enough that the Romans got no inkling of what he was up to, or (more likely, as they were allies) the Romans simply did not understand what was going on.

That pro-Roman warlord died just about the time that a Carthaginian general named Hannibal (heard of him? with the elephants?) was running wild on the Italian mainland with a large force, wiping out one Roman army after another. Leaderless, Syracuse fell to an anti-Roman coup—and the Romans immediately sent a large expedition to retake it.

Three ancient sources fundamentally agree on what happened next (Polybius, writing about 110 BC; Livy, writing in the time of Augustus Caesar; and Plutarch, writing about AD 100).

The Romans launched simultaneous land and sea attacks. Both were repelled before they even got to the walls by a rain of fantastically accurate and rapid missile fire, including quarter-ton rocks. Modern analysts take this as evidence of exquisitely calibrated catapults with central fire control using accurate range-finders.

So the Romans tried again, with night attacks, and did get to the walls despite the unending missile fire.

It was then that things got interesting.

The naval attack involved 100-ton Roman galleys that were more than 120 feet long, with crews of 400 including rowers (who weren't slaves—forget *Ben-Hur.*) These galleys were supposed to rush a section of the city wall that fronted the sea, where Roman marines would swarm over the wall from towers mounted on the galleys. (Yes, the Romans had marines. How did you think they founded an empire?)

As the galleys got to the walls, enormous machines reared up on the other side of the wall, and extended huge poles over the water.

In some cases the machines dropped large weights from the ends of the poles onto the Roman galleys, smashing through their hulls and wrecking them.

In other cases they dropped grappling hooks. Once the hooks snagged a galley, they would literally reel it in. If they had snagged either side of the hull, lifting it would tilt the vessel until it capsized. If they snagged the bow or stern, lifting it would swamp the other end.

In some cases galleys were lifted completely out of the water and left to spin in the air until the crew was tossed to their deaths.

Similar (but presumably smaller) engines were also at work on the land side, picking up individual infantrymen and fatally tossing them about.

Apparently, Syracuse's defenders (led by Archimedes) had built machines that resembled modern tower-style construction cranes, with horizontal booms atop vertical masts. Lacking modern engines, they must have been deployed and then powered using drop-weights in arrangements of Rube Goldberg complexity. (Simply lining the top of the wall with cargo cranes like those used in ancient harbors, as some modern writers assume, would have involved no element of surprise because the cranes would have been standing in plain sight. Nor could such cargo cranes have lifted the galleys clear of the water.)

So how did Archimedes (alone among pre-moderns) design and then replicate such huge machines, which worked so beautifully from the word *go*? Barring a time-machine excursion, Archimedes never saw a modern construction crane. In fact, had he seen one, he might have been discouraged by his own lack of an equivalent power source.

The simplest answer is that Archimedes was that rare case of a genius with full government backing. The word *genius* is not used lightly—next time you see a lever or screw in use, think of him. For that matter, next time you see a mechanical object that was designed using a mathematical model to predict its behavior (and these days, that's everything), think of him.

But there was no comic book ending. The Romans fled—but then got over their panic and laid siege to the city, hoping to starve the thing they could not fight. At some point the junta in Syracuse tried to raise the spirits of its solders by issuing a full wine ration during a festival, even through food remained scarce. The Romans then managed to take a section of the city wall from its groggy defenders. They found the city subdivided by more walls, and spent months taking it section by section amidst the usual famine, plague, brutality, and frenzied looting.

Archimedes died during the looting of the final neighborhood to fall. There are several stories about what happened, but apparently he did not give an appropriate answer to the Roman solder who confronted him.

As for his machines, they are never mentioned again. If the Romans had any use for them, it was for kindling. Probably too much operator skill was involved for their taste.

4
Romans Versus Death Rays

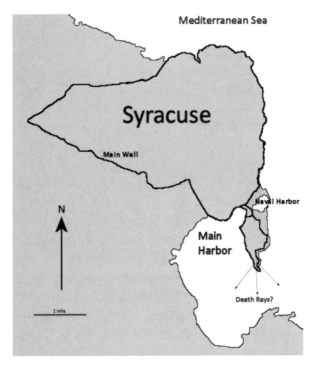

Outline map of Syracuse in 214 BC, showing how Archimedes might have used "death rays" to guard the city's harbor entrance. Map by the author.

As you're aware from the previous chapter, the siege of Syracuse in 214 BC is famous for the well-attested presence of mysterious, huge war machines that panicked the Roman attackers. The whole thing seems like something out of science fiction, but appears to have actually happened, constituting a classic case of a reverse anachronism of the second kind (that is, from the future) turning into a reverse anachronism from the present. The Romans could not understand what they were seeing, because it was from their future, but we have such things (cranes) in our present, and understand what the ancient writers were talking about.

And now we get to the fact that the siege of Syracuse was also famous for the pioneering use of death rays.

No kidding, death rays. But we also have to face the fact that the documentary evidence for Archimedes' death rays is much slipperier than with the previously considered war machines.

Fragmentary references from writers in about AD 170 and AD 500 have led to breathless suppositions, from the Middle Ages to the present, that Archimedes used reflected, focused sunlight as an incendiary weapon against the Romans.

Yet, for all the billions we pour into military research, we still can't get something similar to work.

The simplest explanation is that Archimedes couldn't get it to work either—at least not as a lethal weapon. First, you'll note that the informants were writing about 400 and 700 years after the event, and had no more first-hand knowledge of the siege than we do. Second, you'd think that death rays would be the first thing the Romans would have mentioned, after abandoning the siege and fleeing all the way back to Rome. But the primary sources (Polybius, Livy, and Plutarch) mention no such thing.

Various attempts have been made in modern times to replicate what is assumed to have been Archimedes' death ray, including one by the Greek navy in 1972 and one by the *MythBusters* TV program in 2005. Both used billboard-sized arrays of polished metal mirrors such as Archimedes would have had access to. The former, focused at 50 meters, successfully started a fire. The latter, focused at 30 meters, mostly produced charring.

Both demonstrations involved a target that was well within catapult, arrow, even slingshot range, begging the question, why bother?

But this does not mean that Archimedes—who at one point wrote a treatise on parabolic shapes such as would be useful for mirrors—did not try something with reflected sunlight. Only setting fire to Roman ships may not have been the point.

Consider: there was a time (the present, actually) when celebrities and movie stars cavorting on the beaches of high-dollar resorts on the coast of Mexico could depend on the management to deploy people to stand on the beach with large mirrors, to reflect sunlight into the faces of the pestilential paparazzi gathered in boats just beyond the surf. This disrupts their surveillance, ruins their photos, and gives them migraines.

This cavorting takes place in the vicinity of Cabo San Lucas, on the southern tip of Baja California. The point is that the beach faces south and is in the northern hemisphere, meaning you could catch the sun about any time during daylight.

Syracuse is likewise in the northern hemisphere. It had two harbors (the large main harbor and a small naval harbor), and the mouths of both included a commanding spot facing south on which they could have mounted mirrors. Dazzling the Roman picket boats could facilitate blockade-running in and out of the harbors. Instead of having to wait for night and the navigation dangers presented by darkness, you can sortie during the day after blinding the enemy enough to get a head start. The dazzled enemy ship might even run aground. Setting an enemy ship ablaze would be an added bonus, of course.

That may be the simplest explanation of what Archimedes was doing with mirrors, assuming he was doing anything. But while the simplest explanation is always the one to bet on, admittedly it is not always the correct one.

Another possibility is that the death-ray sources are actually correct, but that solar mirrors, with their well-attested limitations, were not involved. That would mean the use of some other kind of energy beam. But we would have to assume that it was one that did not involve a modernistic, complex, heavy-metal infrastructure for the generation, storage, and transmission of electricity, which would have left plenty of evidence. We'll further assume that the ancient historians did not mention it because they did not understand one iota of what was going on and ascribed whatever happened to bad weather.

It may be far-fetched, but remember—we're dealing with Archimedes.

So, if the death-ray stories are true, we must be dealing with another reverse anachronism of the second kind. In other words, because it properly belongs in our future, we can't figure it out.

Time will tell (literally).

5
Roman Steam Engines

Sketch of one type of aeolipile, or Roman-era steam engine.
NASA/nasaimages.org.

The Industrial Revolution was based on steam engines and the unprecedented power they offered. The first practical steam engine with an established market was the Newcomen engine of 1712, in which expanding steam raised a piston in a cylinder. A mist of cool water then condensed the steam under the piston, creating a vacuum, which sucked down the piston, generating the power stroke. In 1774 the Watt engine appeared on the market, with steam generated in a separate boiler and piped to the cylinder, where it was

31

valved to one side and then the other to drive the piston back and forth. These were large machines operating at low pressures, suitable for mines and factories. Smaller, high-pressure versions were in circulation by 1800, permitting the use of steamships and locomotives, and the enormous advantages they offered over sailing ships and wagons pulled by draft animals. Enormous economic expansion became possible as goods moved cheaply.

Yes, it's a satisfying story, especially with its comforting implication that progress is the inevitable result of applied science and technology. So it's a little disquieting to discover that the Greeks and Romans had steam engines, too, and the results were not what anyone would call progress. Instead, it's more of a case of items out of space and time that hide in plain sight.

The smoking gun is a treatise titled "Pneumatics," by Hero of Alexandria, written in about AD 60. (Although Alexandria is in Egypt, Hero is usually referred to as Greek rather than Egyptian.) It described dozens of little machines powered by compressed air or flowing water, to do things like blow a horn when a door is opened. Most are intended for use in Greek temples. He does not come out and say that the devices are intended to awe credulous worshipers by performing little "miracles" on command, but that's the impression. Other devices, however, seem to exist pretty much for their own sakes.

The device in Chapter 50 appears to be one of the latter. It was called an aeolipile, from Aeolus (Greek god of the wind) and *pila* (Latin for "ball"). Hero called for the fairly complicated construction of a covered cauldron with pipes going up from its lid into opposite sides of a metal ball. The ball would be able to spin on those pipes, which would serve as the ball's axis of rotation, as if they were the supports on the poles of a globe. From the middle of the ball (or the globe's equator, to continue the analogy) would come two outlet pipes bent in opposite directions along the equator. When the water in the cauldron was brought to a boil, steam would travel through the inlet pipes and into the ball, and then out of the outlet pipes, causing the ball to spin.

So you have a steam turbine. With a belt it could turn something else, such as a small pump. You could not call it efficient, but as long as you kept the fire going and refilled the cauldron with water, you could keep your aeolipile spinning indefinitely. But Hero makes no mention of any such utilization— a spinning ball was the whole point, apparently.

In 25 BC, 85 years earlier, the Roman building manual "De Architectura" by Vitruvius (who may have been a catapult artilleryman in Julius Caesar's army) spent a paragraph in Chapter VI of Book I describing aeolipiles.

Vitruvius described them as hollow bronze balls with one small opening. You pour water in them and put them by a fire, and when the water boils you'll see a dramatic demonstration of how nature creates wind through a combination of heat and moisture.

He was not describing aeolipiles for their own sakes, but was using them to underscore his point that moving air is a force to be reckoned with (and that towns ought to be laid out so that the citizens will not be exposed to prevailing winds blowing down the length of the main street). But he surely would not have tossed out such a casual reference to aeolipiles unless he was confident that his readers were familiar with them.

In other words, we can assume that crude little steam engines were a common fixture in the life of a literate Roman, either as self-propelled toys or as spectacles at a temple. With two unconnected references to them 85 years apart, we can assume that more was going on, and that some people had found actual uses for them.

So why didn't the Romans take the next obvious step, and expand the idea for industrial applications? The most common answer is that they had slave labor and/or high unemployment, and therefore were not on the lookout for labor-saving innovations.

There's an anecdote about the Roman emperor Vespasian (AD 9–79) related by the Roman historian Suetonius, who was himself born about the time Vespasian died. Besides endangering himself early in his career by falling asleep during stage performances by then-emperor Nero, and causing a ruckus after his enthronement by insisting he did not need help getting his boots off, Vespasian was famous as a tightwad, not recoiling from taxing public urinals. (They were a source of ammonia used by laundries.) But Suetonius noted that, nonetheless, Vespasian handsomely supported quite a few intellectuals. Then Suetonius slipped in this sentence: "Mechanico quoque grandis columnas exigua impensa perducturum in Capitolium pollicenti praemium pro commento non mediocre optulit, operam remisit praefatus sineret se plebiculam pascere." In other words, "To a mechanical engineer, who promised to transport some heavy columns to the Capitol at little expense, he gave no small reward for his invention, but refused to use it, saying that the poor must eat."

Presumably he would have reacted to steam engines the same way (assuming the invention in question was not actually a steam engine). But keep in mind that employment is not always an issue. Those first steam engines in England in 1712 were used to pump water out of mines, where the confined spaces made a reliance on muscle power impractical. The Romans would have appreciated the same advantage.

On the other hand, those mines where the British installed the first steam engines were coal mines, and the coal they produced could be used to run the engines. The Romans did not have coal mines, and relied on firewood. Any reliance on steam power would have contributed to deforestation, or at least the fuel would have been seen as a significant expense.

Meanwhile, the Romans' metallurgy was not that great, and this is sometimes cited as a factor. But the same could have been said about British metallurgy in 1712. In England, steam engines and metallurgy fed off each other and advanced in parallel, and that also could have happened in Rome. The Romans certainly figured out how to build intricate metal mechanisms, as shown in Chapter 3.

The real answer probably has nothing to do with technology, but culture. The Romans built fine ships, ports, buildings, and roads in much the same way, for centuries. We should probably not be comparing the Romans with 18th-century England, but with imperial China. The latter's craftspeople were every bit as skilled as their Roman counterparts, but they, too, carried on for centuries without mounting an industrial revolution.

Basically, it seems fair to say that in both cases the "dominant culture" was uninterested in innovations. They especially were not interested in innovations that would let random people get uppity and enrich themselves in defiance of their prescribed place in the social order.

And so they gawked at the spinning steam turbine, which was probably turned on during a sermon about the power and glory of the god Aeolus. Then they genuflected and moved on, dropping coins in a box by the exit.

A better question is: what are we gawking at today? What cultural blind spot prevents us from taking advantage of the thing that would open the door to the next revolution that would vastly improve human life? What is hiding in plain sight in front of us?

Let's hope it doesn't take 20 centuries to get an answer.

6
The *Hunley*

Sketch of the CSS Hunley, *whose eerily modern appearance belied the fact that it was built in 1863. Public domain image from Wikimedia Commons.*

It seems eerily modern. It had conning towers, a metal hull, dive planes, and ballast tanks. It was driven by a propeller, and carried a torpedo. At first glance it has a great deal in common with the several thousand military submarines built for the world's navies since the first commissioned submarine, the U.S. Navy's SS-1, in 1900.

It was built in 1863, with no benefit of later technology. It worked, and managed to sortie into the ocean under its own power and sink an enemy vessel. It was the first submarine to ever do that. But it was also the first submarine to sink twice during training and drown its crew both times. So it may be fairer to say that it barely worked, illustrating the dangers of prematurely relying on new technology. In fact, its owners may have been better off had it not worked at all, causing them to abandon the project and go on to something else.

We're talking about the *Hunley*, a 40-foot 7-ton submarine operated by the Confederate navy from the port of Charleston during the U.S. Civil War. The idea behind it was to launch stealth attacks against the U.S. Navy vessels that were blockading the port and cutting off the rebellious Confederacy from vital imports. Ending the blockade would have greatly improved the Confederacy's survival chances.

It was not the first submarine ever built—people had been tinkering with the idea since the ancient Greeks, but the results mostly emphasized the advantages of using watercraft that floated. Aside from the lack of visibility after submerging, the only available power sources were wind and oars, and neither were much help underwater.

By the time of the U.S. Civil War, marine engineers also had steam power and propellers. Steam was impractical in a confined unventilated space underwater, but propellers worked where oars didn't. So a hand-cranked propeller was seized as the solution.

There were probably a couple dozen such submarines built during the war, and all proved to be sadly underpowered. The problem is that a man can sustain an output of about one-tenth horsepower (although a trained athlete can do much better in spurts). So even if you harnessed a whole squad you only have one horsepower, and you'll be happy to move at a pace equivalent to a relaxed stroll. Meanwhile, the crew used oxygen while frantically cranking, limiting the craft's underwater range—and putting them at risk of blacking out as the limit was approached.

One of the earliest examples was actually operated by the U.S. Navy. The 47-foot *Alligator*, with a crew of 12, was on its way to Charleston in April 1863, to undertake underwater demolition missions against the rebel port. It sank in a storm while being towed through the Atlantic, but no one was on board so no one was lost.

The same cannot be said for the *Hunley*. Its builders (led by Louisiana engineer Horace Lawson Hunley, hence the name of the boat) tried building a machine in New Orleans, and another in Mobile Bay, before shifting to Charleston. They tried steam and electrical propulsion before settling on muscle. The craft was made out of iron plates and was often mistaken for a rebuilt steam boiler, but was actually custom-made with appropriate streamlining. It was operated by a crew of eight (or sometimes nine).

The hull was only about four feet wide and being inside must have been like crouching inside a drainage culvert. There were small conning towers near the front and rear. The commander sat under the front one, steered, operated the diving planes, and operated the hand pump that controlled the front ballast tank. The crewman under the rear conning tower handled the pump for the rear ballast tank. The rest of the crew sat between them along a bench, turning a crank geared to the propeller.

The conning towers, 8 inches high, were only large enough to contain portholes. Each was topped with an entry hatch that was only about 14 x 16 inches, which was troublesome for anyone with wide shoulders—or was in a hurry to escape drowning.

The Confederate crew started training in the submarine in Charleston harbor in early August 1863. While moving on the surface on August 29 the boat suddenly submerged while the hatches were open. Three (some say four) of the crew managed to get out, while five drowned. The Confederates dragged it to the surface, drained out the water, removed the bodies, recruited replacements, and carried on.

Hunley (although a civilian) took over command after that. He was conducting a submerged practice attack on October 15 when the submarine failed to return to the surface. Hunley apparently forgot to close the inlet valve for the front ballast tank. The tank was really a basin—it had no top—and the hull quickly flooded. Hunley, and the man who operated the rear pump, suffocated with their heads in the air pockets that formed in the conning towers. They were apparently trying to push the hatches open, which was impossible against the water pressure. In the hull between them the rest of the crew drowned.

Divers found the hull three weeks later, its nose buried in the bottom of the harbor at a steep angle. They dragged it to the surface, drained out the water, removed the bodies, recruited replacements, and carried on.

This time, however, they were under orders to remain on the surface. Of course the hull was awash in anything by glassy calm, so the difference may have been academic. But the new crew managed to learn how to operate the boat, and survive, until February 17, 1864. It was a moonlit night and the USS *Housatonic* had gotten into the habit of spending the hours of darkness in a spot where it covered the northern approach channel that blockade runners used for darting into the port. The spot was close enough inshore for a round-trip sortie by the *Hunley*.

The *Hunley* was armed with what they called a torpedo and which we would call a cask of gunpowder on a long pole with a barbed point, protruding from the front of the hull. The idea was to ram the point into an enemy ship and then back away. A cord attached to the cask would unreel from a spool on the *Hunley*'s hull. After the cord was fully unreeled it would go taut and pull a trigger on the cask, detonating it and sinking the enemy.

That night the crew of the *Housatonic* reported seeing a long, narrow object approach them at or just under the surface, moving at 3 or 4 knots. They were only able to fire small arms at it before the explosion occurred. All but five of the *Housatonic*'s crew managed to climb into the rigging as the ship settled to the bottom of the shallow water.

The *Hunley* did not return. Somewhere on the way back it had gone down for the third and last time.

The location of the hull was confirmed in 1995, and it was raised in 2000. Examinations continue, but there was no obvious damage to explain the sinking. The remains of the crew were found at their posts, which would not be the case if they had been trying to escape. Perhaps they decided to lay on the bottom to avoid the enemy vessels that swarmed to the area. There, cold and hypoxia gradually—even comfortably—did their work.

Obviously, the *Hunley* represents a case of bleeding-edge technology. They eventually got the submarine to work as desired, but in total it killed more friendly personnel (21) than enemy personnel (5). Considered as a naval war the tradeoff was more favorable, with 7 Confederate tons lost to 1,200 Union tons.

The Hunley is also an eerie reverse anachronism, in that it is about what you'd expect a modern engineer would produce if he or she were sent back to 1863 and was told to design a submarine. Aside from taller and wider conning towers supporting bigger entry hatches (better nutrition, you understand) there would be only two major design alterations:

The first would involve enclosing the ballast tanks, turning them into actual tanks instead of basins. This would end the danger of accidental flooding through ballast inlet valves (which killed the second crew).

The other would involve harnessing something other than muscle power. The steam and electrical power the *Hunley* experimented with were indeed impractical in 1863. However, compressed air was not, and the French navy was at that same time building a submarine powered by compressed air, called the *Plongeur*. It had about the speed and range of the *Hunley*, but was much bigger, with a 12-man crew.

The first unmanned self-propelled anti-ship underwater projectiles (that is, torpedoes in the modern sense) appeared at almost the same time, in 1866, in the Austro-Hungarian navy. These, too, were powered by compressed air, with a range of a thousand yards at 6 knots.

So, in theory, it would have been possible for an anachronistic engineer, who knew then what is known now, to produce a version of the *Hunley* with enough horsepower (more than one horsepower, anyway) to operate reliably and effectively against the blockaders. This could have been destabilizing weapon. It could have changed history.

But that would have meant a Confederate victory. So it is also possible that someone who knew then what is known now would choose not to build it.

7
Steam-Age Computer Revolution

Modern re-creation of Babbage's Difference Engine No. 2 being readied at a museum in London. Science Museum/SSPL. Used with permission.

They would use punched cards to feed in data—thousands, if necessary, because complexity would not matter as long as the programming was correct. There would be machine memory for the data and for the program. The machine could perform loops and conditional jumps, and evaluate if-then-else statements. A special printer would produce the results. Yes, all the fundamentals of a modern computer had come together in 1842.

Yes, there was an 8 in that date.

Today's electronic computers trace their ancestry to the programmable electronic calculating devices developed during and immediately following World War II, including the Colossus, the ENIAC, and the EDVAC. So if the lead paragraph had said 1942, you'd be feeling no mental dissonance. But as it turns out, a full century before that time a small group in England did their best to invent a computer, using purely mechanical technology. It's as if they were yearning for something that they could dimly sense but could not quite express.

They almost succeeded, leaving us with some marvelous what-ifs. Meanwhile, modern analysis indicates that they failed due to bureaucratic and project management deficiencies, and not because of any flaw in the technology they developed.

The story of steam-age computer science centers around Charles Babbage (1791–1871), a well-to-do academic and mathematician. He's often depicted as a crank, thanks to his failed efforts to get elected to Parliament and his personal crusades against noisy organ grinders and boys frightening horses by playing hoop-rolling in the streets. But cranks aren't consulted by major railroads or appointed as the Lucasian Professor of Mathematics at Cambridge, a chair he held from 1828 to 1839. (One of his predecessors was Isaac Newton. One of his successors was Stephen Hawking.)

His calling as a mathematician led to another of his crusades, involving errata for mathematical tables. In the absence of computational devices, the endless calculations required for navigation, engineering, and finance would have been impractical without the ability to look up intermediate results in various kinds of math tables. These were printed in special books, and Babbage had a collection of about 300.

However, the table values were calculated by hand, they were transcribed by hand, and the books were set in type by hand. Each step was subject to errors—errors that editors found hard to spot in what were, to the eye, rows and columns of arbitrary numbers. But a calculation that used an erroneous table entry would itself produce an erroneous result. Major publishers not only produced errata sheets of the errors in their tables, but errata sheets of errors in the original errata sheets, and then errata sheets of the errors in the errata sheets of the original errata sheets. One analysis of 40 books of math tables found 3,700 known errors. The number of unknown errors was, of course, unknown.

But during his lifetime Babbage saw machinery being applied to wider and wider uses. Maybe machinery could also be applied to this problem?

So he began work in 1821 on a project he called the Difference Engine, a hand-cranked device that would calculate table entries, print them, and set the type for them, all without error-prone human intervention. The name derived from the machine's use of the method of finite differences to calculate results. The method used repetitive addition and subtraction, which was easier to mechanize than multiplication and division.

According to the plans, it would have taken 25,000 parts, weighed 15 tons, and been 8 feet high, 7 feet long, and 3 feet wide. Babbage finagled substantial government funding for its development, and part of it was assembled by 1832, despite Babbage's partial breakdown in 1827 when his wife, father, and one child (of eight) died within a few months of each other.

But in 1833 the project ground to a stop when his head mechanic walked away after a dispute over expenses—the man relocated his shop to be closer to Babbage but Babbage would not pay for it. Government funding dried up about that time as the bureaucrats lost patience.

Babbage, however, remained smitten with the idea of automated calculations, and proceeded to expand his idea into a fully programmable general purpose machine with separate storage for a program and for data. He called it the Analytical Engine. This is the machine mentioned previously, with punched cards for programming, and a processing unit that could perform loops and conditional jumps. The Difference Engine became part of the processor. The Analytical Engine was fully described by 1842. Babbage anticipated that it could perform additions or subtractions at a rate of one per second. Multiplication and division would take a full minute for two 50-digit numbers. It would have covered a tennis court and probably required steam power to operate.

He never seriously sought funding for it, although he did tinker with some components. But the effort did lead him to redesign and simplify the Difference Engine. No. 2 had about one third the parts of its predecessor.

Two copies of Difference Engine No. 2 have since been built, starting in 1985. There was some concern (shared by Babbage) that the file-and-fit production methods available during his time could not have produced metal parts with the necessary precision. The modern machines were intentionally built with 19th-century tolerances, but worked fine from the moment the crank was turned.

In other words, with a little more patience, time, and money Babbage could have gotten his machines to work—presumably even the Analytical Machine. There are historical fiction genres devoted to speculating about what changes its use would have brought to the Victorian world, but we have to keep in mind that this was a mainframe, not a personal computer. It was personal computers with high-speed communications that produced the digital revolution in the 20th century. It's hard to envision a personal version of the Analytical Engine. And when its development began, "high-speed communications" meant semaphore towers, and there was nothing personal about them, either.

Beyond that, Babbage's machine was designed for computation, not data storage and retrieval. It might have made the calculation of government pension benefits more precise, but it was not intended to, say, store files on every citizen and then look for population trends. Nothing like that would be attempted until the U.S. census of 1890, and would involve crude electromechanical tabulating machines rather than mechanical computers.

Still, Babbage was aiming for something that seems startlingly modern. But assuming some time traveler did inspire Babbage, he or she did a poor job telling Babbage how to make a computer, because, ironically, Babbage's Analytical Engine was in many ways more complicated than a modern computer. Babbage used decimal numbers and performed decimal arithmetic operations with them, which demands complex machinery. Modern computers use binary numbers, and binary math is trivial and lends itself to being expressed through on-off electrical circuits. Babbage used separate storage for data, instructions, and math table entries, whereas modern computers use main memory for all three. Meanwhile, Babbage made no allowance for the processing of text, which is indispensible for a modern computer. However, that does not mean that a way could not have been found.

Babbage and his machine clearly were reverse anachronisms, but ones that speak to a phenomenon that became clear only with the invention of the microprocessor and the runaway success of the personal computer: People have an insatiable hunger for computational power. If the power is there, people will find a use for it, freeing themselves from the intellectual limitations imposed by the drudgery of arithmetic, and replacing the vagaries of memory with the surety of information retrieval. Babbage likewise felt the need for such power in his anti-errata crusade, but was one of the first people in history who clearly saw some way to acquire it.

Yet, the Analytical Machine may yet turn out to be a reverse anachronism from the future, as Babbage's approach may prove to be the salvation of the computer industry—someday. Heat problems have caused processor speeds to top out at around four billion cycles per second—with electronic devices. But nanotechnology may eventually allow us to build the mechanical Analytical

Engine (or its binary equivalent) at a molecular scale. Being mechanical it would not be subject to the same heat problems, and being tiny it could run at lightning speeds.

Babbage would have loved it.

BUILDINGS

In a world of uncertainty, you'd think buildings and monuments would offer something real and unambiguous. Someone has to have built them, after all. Indeed, for any given building, there are there are four things you'd expect to know about it:

1. Who built it.
2. Why.
3. How.
4. When.

But it turns out that, with some of the most famous buildings on Earth, two out of four ain't bad. For the rest of the answers, we're left with conjectures and creation myths.

And if we try to get past the conjectures and myths, things get really weird. It turns out that the best-preserved building from ancient Rome was built with methods and materials that we would consider modern. Also, it served no purpose or function that can now be identified. Meanwhile, we can go to the moon, but the ancient Athenians erected a building that we couldn't duplicate to save our lives. And, of course, we have no real information about why they built it that way. As for the Sphinx in Egypt, it may be that everything we thought we knew about is wrong, including the name.

How can this be? Clearly there is no one answer. But the questions are fascinating. Read on.

8
The Parthenon

Built 24 centuries ago, the Parthenon in Athens has features that we do not understand, and which we would have great difficulty replicating. Wikimedia Commons image by user Onkel Tuca. Used under license.

Pretend you're socially prominent enough to be included on a committee empowered to erect a building that is important to your religion. Additionally, the building is expected to serve as a showpiece for your culture and a symbol of your government's power and prosperity—and its recovery after a recent military defeat. The building's holiness demands mathematical precision in its execution, but the architect reminds the committee that executing the calculated dimensions with total precision would actually be counterproductive. After all, the long straight and parallel lines of the sacred geometry will not be perceived as straight and parallel by the curved human eyeball. So it is traditional to make the supporting columns taper from the bottom, so they will look rectilinear when they actually aren't.

And that's when you speak up. Tinkering with the columns is not good enough in this case, you insist. The slap-dash way they apply visual refinements in temples in one-horse city-states along the periphery won't do here.

Here, we're going all out. Nothing must prevent the sacred geometry from prevailing over the human eyeball. Therefore, the building must not have a single straight line—horizontal or vertical. The foundation of the building should hump upward toward the middle. The columns should lean inward slightly. And it is not enough that they should taper—they should swell delicately toward the middle.

That will mean that not one single block of stone in the building will be a straight-sided rectangle. The shape of every one will have to be carefully and individually sculpted, based on a sophisticated understanding of geometry. But they need to fit together so well that no mortar is needed. Yes, construction costs will be sky-high. So?

Such a meeting took place in Athens in 447 BC. The project was green-lighted, and 16 years later they had the Parthenon, still considered the finest architectural expression of the Greek golden age, if not of Western civilization. It incorporates endless visual refinements. Because we don't actually have the minutes of the steering committee meeting for the Parthenon, or for other temples that used varying degrees of similar refinements, we don't really know what the point was. But, as speculated, the builders appeared to assume that it was important to achieve some sort of visual perfection that transcended the imperfections of vision. As to how they calculated the refinements, we really don't know either, but whatever they did, it worked.

Measuring 228 feet long and 101 feet wide, with Doric-style columns 34 feet high, the Parthenon is located on the acropolis of Athens, the 500-foot-high rocky plateau in the middle of the city that once served as a fortress. Like most Greek temples it was intended to be viewed from all sides. And from all sides you would see a row of marble columns holding up a marble roof. The space between the roof supports and the actual roof was lined with elaborate statues. Many of these were difficult to see from the ground, but that was not considered an issue—the Olympian gods could see them. Inside the row of columns, under the roof, was a walled inner sanctuary, whose walls were also heavily decorated.

From a distance, the building looks perfectly proportioned and rectilinear. That's an illusion. Along the short sides, the floors hump upward a little more than 2.5 inches toward the middle. Along the long side they hump up more than 4 inches. The roof line has the same curvature, as the columns are all the same height. The columns swell toward the middle by about 7/10 of an inch for the outer row of columns. The inner columns swell about one inch and the swelling peaks a little above the middle. Meanwhile, the columns lean inward slightly, and if they were tall enough they would converge at a point about a mile above the building. Yes, some of these refinements are delicate and subtle, but they are consistent and obviously intentional. The effort involved must have been immense—yet the results were intended to be unnoticed.

Anyway, that's what we do know. After that we get deeper and deeper into mysteries.

The first and most mundane mystery is the name. *Parthenon* means "property of the virgins" in Greek and may have referred to some type of priestess, but the variety of theories behind the name underscore our ignorance. Presumably it was a nickname. Early writers refer to it as "the 100-foot-building."

And then there's the use of the building. Officially it was a temple of Athena, patron goddess of ancient Athens, and its inner sanctuary housed a gold and ivory statue of the goddess. But it could not really have been a temple because the statue's gold was removable and was part of the state treasury. The fact that the statue could be dismantled without sacrilege indicates that the statue was not itself dedicated to cult worship—that apparently took place elsewhere. Perhaps it was a sort of Fort Knox that was open to tourists.

Then there was a question of how they built it, considering that surveying at that time was based on taut string. Making a large building with precisely straight corners and lines was demanding enough, but the Parthenon required corners and lines that were precisely not-quite-straight. At other ancient Greek building sites researchers have found flat surfaces with incised one-to-one scale schematics of architectural elements, so maybe the Parthenon's builders had something similar.

Finally, there's the question of why. Why were they so fixated on architectural optical illusions? Why were they so intent on adding expensive visual refinements that would make the building look rectilinear? It would have looked almost as rectilinear if it actually were rectilinear.

For centuries it was assumed that the Greeks had made a fetish of the golden ratio, and didn't want the human eyeball to get in the way of its expression. In designs involving the golden ratio you have two lines, or two sides of a rectangle, A and B, so that A plus B all divided by A happens to be equal to A divided by B. It implies a ratio of about 1.62 between A and B.

Alas, modern scholarship tends to shoot this down, as the golden ratio did not get popular until about a century after the Parthenon was built. Yes, you can find the ratio in measurements of the building—if you carefully choose what you measure. The same is probably true of the Empire State Building.

So we don't know what the big deal was. We just know that it was a big deal—to them.

Converted to a church and then a mosque, the building remained in use and largely intact until 1687. Then, when it was about 20 centuries old, it was used as an ammo depot by an Ottoman garrison that was besieged by a force from Venice. A Venetian shell set off the stored ammo, wrecking the building, bringing down the roof, and knocking down the walls of the inner sanctuary and some columns. Some of the surviving statues were carried off by an English nobleman in about 1810, and they have become a bone of contention between the Greek and British governments. As for the ruins of the building itself, the last century has seen increasing efforts to restore what's left and prevent further deterioration.

A full-scale replica of the intact Parthenon has been built (and rebuilt) in Nashville, Tennessee, during the last century. It preserves the Parthenon's visual refinements, but not the original building methods, as the structural elements are made of efficiently cast, visually uninteresting concrete, with sealed joints between them. The Parthenon, of course, is made of precisely fitted blocks of translucent marble.

And maybe that difference highlights the gulf that separates us from the Parthenon. We may not be able to understand the Parthenon until we reach a point where the aesthetic embodied in a building's appearance and construction is considered at least as important as its use. And maybe that's not as touchy-feely as it sounds. As long as it manages to stand upright and keep out the weather, a building can be put to any use that satisfies the transitory whim of its owner. But its appearance lives on regardless of use, to bore or amaze the onlooker. And the nature of its construction lives on to, likewise, bore or amaze the on-looker. And if it manages to amaze, then the mysteries embodied in its appearance and construction continue to inspire.

We're not there yet. We can't say that the Parthenon is some kind of reverse anachronism from the present, because we have only cheap imitations. If it is one from the future, it is from the far future indeed.

9
The Pantheon

The best preserved ancient building in the world, the Pantheon in Rome was built with modern methods, and served no obvious purpose. Wikimedia Commons image by Remi Jouan. Used under license.

If you want to nominate something as the foundation of modern civilization, look no further than concrete. The floor below you is likely made out of it, as are major roads, drainage facilities, dams, airports, and ports. The availability of quality building stone (which would otherwise be a limiting factor) is immaterial because with concrete you can make your own building stone, on site, in any shape necessary. The critical component—cement powder—was first patented in England in 1796, and its use spread hand-in-hand with the Industrial Revolution.

At least that's the story—it's a tidy story, and the facts do check out. But if you go to Rome you can see a remarkably preserved building called the Pantheon that is known to have been built in AD 126.

It's made out of concrete.

It doesn't stop there. Many buildings erected after Nero's fire in AD 64 were concrete faced with bricks. The surviving ruins of the 33-acre Baths of Caracalla, a Roman leisure center and shopping mall built in AD 212, are concrete. Parts of the famous Roman aqueduct system were made of concrete. Port facilities of Caesarea Maritima, a Roman city on the coast of what is now Israel whose construction began in 13 BC, were made of special concrete designed to harden under water. Numerous Roman fortifications were based on concrete.

Apparently, sometime during the Roman Republic the Romans found that if you combined certain kinds of volcanic ash (common in central Italy) with slaked lime (powder resulting from the baking of limestone that is thereupon slaked—or mixed—with water) and let it fully harden (which takes four weeks) the result is like quarried building stone. Except that is superior to quarried stone, because it can be formed in molds, and can be easily shaped into arches and other architectural elements that are problematic if assembled from stones or bricks. Its use was detailed in Chapter 2 of a surviving Roman building manual ("De Architectura," by Vitruvius) written about 25 BC. The discovery appears to have been empirical (that is, from trial and error) rather than from scientific inquiry, which the Romans, frankly, weren't known for. The same book advises against using lead in drinking water pipes, again purely on empirical evidence.

Roman concrete differed from the modern version in important respects. The modern version has more chemical components, and those components are scientifically defined, so there is no reliance on a particular volcanic ash. Modern concrete is usually made wet enough to pump through pipes, whereas the Roman version was mixed with the minimum possible amount of water and then applied by hand. But the biggest difference is that today they lay the wet concrete over steel reinforcing rods, which should make the resulting edifice much stronger. The best the Romans could do was use rubble fill.

And that brings us back to the Pantheon. The best-preserved ancient building on Earth, it's shaped like a squat barrel with a domed roof—basically a free-standing rotunda—with a column-lined front porch that makes it look like a Pagan temple. Its name means "For All the Gods" in Greek, also implying that it was a Pagan temple. Other than that, its status today is the same as the day it was built: It's the world's largest unreinforced concrete dome. The dome is 142 feet high, although the top is pierced with a large open hole called the oculus (eye), and the paved floor below is shaped to drain away any incoming rainwater.

Modern analysis shows that the Pantheon was cleverly built. The thickness of the dome narrows from about 21 feet at the base to a little less than four feet at the oculus. The rubble that was mixed with the cement started at the bottom as dense marble fragments, while at the top they were using light, porous volcanic slag. There is some question whether it could have lasted this long otherwise. And there is some question as to whether anyone attempting a similar project today would dare not to use reinforcing steel.

But, weirdly, beyond engineering details little can be said about the Pantheon with certainty. Roman temples usually face east toward the rising sun, but the Pantheon faces north, and the roof's oculus and the front door are the only light sources. A standard Roman temple would have an inner chamber that housed the cult statue, where sacrifices and ceremonies were performed. (The inner chamber was called a cella, from which we get the word *cell*.) But the dome of the Pantheon just covers a flat, circular, undivided floor. There are some alcoves along the wall that may have housed statues, but there is no sign of a cella.

A Roman historian writing only 75 years after the building was constructed did not mention any purpose for it and could only speculate as to the source of its name—he thought it was because of the statues of multiple gods erected outside it, or because of the domed roof, which, from the inside, looked like the heavens. This would indicate that it was not really a temple—if it was, he would have accepted the name as self-explanatory. (Also, the statues would have been inside, not outside.)

The builders put an inscription over the front entrance, but it turns out to only add to the mystery. It reads: "M·AGRIPPA·L·F·COS·TERTIVM·FECIT," which is abbreviated Latin for "Three-term Consul Marcus Agrippa, son of Lucius, built this." But inscriptions on temples were usually dedications, not credits. Worse yet, the three-term consul that the inscription refers to must have been the Marcus Agrippa who was the son-in-law and adopted heir of Augustus Caesar. (The consul was the constitutional head of state, elected under the Roman Republic, but appointed by the emperor during the later empire.) Agrippa ended the civil wars that followed the assassination of Julius Caesar and turned the Roman Empire into a functional enterprise by defeating the star-crossed lovers and imperial rebels Antony and Cleopatra at the naval battle of Actium in 31 BC. So it is not surprising that his name turns up on a Roman public building. The problem is that he died in 12 BC and the Pantheon was erected in AD 126, so it's clear that he had nothing to do with it, despite the inscription.

Apparently the original Pantheon was built about 27 BC, presumably by Marcus Agrippa himself, but it burned to the ground in AD 80. It was rebuilt, and burned to the ground in AD 110. Its replacement, being concrete, has yet to burn. Presumably, the crediting inscription was carried over from the original to its replacement, and then its replacement, for sentimental, political, or religious reasons. Agrippa turned out to be an ancestor of two later emperors plus various emperors' wives and Roman consuls, so there might have been pressure to keep his building extant.

But why did that building need to be a non-flammable concrete dome of unprecedented size, enclosing, basically, a whole lot of empty space? Tradition has it that the original building was erected as a monument to the Battle of Actium. Perhaps it housed naval trophies, but they would not have survived two fires. And there is nothing nautical about the current building. If it was a memorial, it seems odd there is no inscription saying so. Admittedly, we continue building rotunda nowadays, and their enclosed volumes serve no specific purpose, but at least they add dignity to otherwise sterile capitol buildings or frivolous malls. But the Pantheon connected to no other building.

So the best-preserved ancient building in the world was erected for no obvious reason, yet was built with modern methods.

The Pantheon has since gone on to serve as a church and a tomb, and it's fair to say it's been in continuous use since it was built—assuming, originally, it had a use other than to be big and carry the Agrippa name.

And then there's the other mystery: why was the secret of concrete lost for so many centuries? Presumably it was not an issue of science being lost in the dark ages, as the Roman knowledge of concrete was not based on science—their chemical discoveries were purely empirical. Also, Vitruvius's book was copied and circulated enough that you can't say it was ever lost, although some of the technical jargon probably became inaccessible. It's more likely that times changed and cost-be-damned monumental building programs with compressed schedules, where concrete was essential, became a thing of the past. Quarrying building stone (or recycling material from old buildings) became cheaper than burning lime to make binder. Craftsmen with the necessary skills became hard to assemble. Soon, using concrete was out of the question, and eventually the question itself was forgotten.

In the meantime, almost any building that has a rotunda (including the U.S. and many state capitols) can claim descent from the Pantheon and its dome. One wonders if they will still be around after nearly 19 centuries—and be as mysterious to their beholders. But hopefully they'll still know how to make concrete.

10
The Sphinx

*Everything we thought we knew about the Sphinx may be wrong—
including who built it, when, and why. Wikimedia Commons image
by Berthold Werner. Used under license.*

It reclines on the edge of the Giza Plateau, adjacent to the Great Pyramid, facing east towards the rising sun. Its body is that of a lion, with its front legs outstretched and its rear legs folded under it. Its head (lacking a nose) is that of a man, and is raised and watchful. On the whole, its demeanor is that of a hybrid guard animal. The head wears a pleated headdress similar (but not identical) to that worn by pharaohs—or it could represent a cat's mane. The head is somewhat small in proportion to the body, leading to speculation that it was once a feline head that was later chipped down and reworked into a human head.

And that's about all we can say for certain about the Sphinx of Giza. It turns out that we can't say who built it, when, or why. The textbooks repeat an assumption that the pyramid builders were responsible for it, but the evidence for that is hardly better than the evidence cited by some fringe theories. Indeed, there are some who insist that it does not fit into Egyptian history as we know it.

Wherever it came from, it is the largest statue in the world made from a single piece of stone. Basically, it's an improved limestone outcropping 241 feet long, 20 feet wide, and 66 feet high. The outline was improved with stone masonry.

Due to its proximity to the pyramids, it is easy to assume that it was built during the 4th Dynasty (2613 to 2494 BC) when pyramid-building on Giza was at full tilt. Remnants of that era, such as ruined mortuary temples and roads, are shoe-horned around it.

Better yet, the so-called Dream Stele was found sitting between its front paws when some sand was removed in 1816. (The rest of the sand was not entirely cleared away until the 1930s.) This flat stone slab included a hieroglyphic inscription purporting to be an announcement by Pharaoh Thutmose IV. Erected during the first year of his reign (about 1401 BC), it tells of him falling asleep in the shadow of the Sphinx while hunting in the vicinity while he was still a prince. The Sphinx (or an associated god) then came to him in a dream asking him to dig away the sand and restore the statue, which the prince thereupon did. It refers to the Sphinx as being associated with 4th Dynasty Pharaoh Khafra, builder of the second largest pyramid at Giza.

So the huge statue is just another artifact of the 4th Dynasty's monumental building craze—until you look closer.

Revisionists point out that the 4th Dynasty ruins around the Sphinx were apparently shoe-horned around it because they were built later. Had they been built at the same time they would surely have shared some rational layout. The Dream Stele, meanwhile, is so damaged that they can't be sure that it truly mentions Khafra. If it does, there's no surviving text on the stele linking him to the Sphinx or anything else. All the stele really tells us is that the Sphinx was a mysterious antiquity in 1401 BC. Meanwhile, no earlier inscription in Egypt mentions the Sphinx.

Especially destructive to the textbook theory are the marks of obvious water erosion on parts of the statue, indicating that it has been exposed to running water for extended periods. However, the region was dry before the last ice age about 13,000 years ago, became wet during the ice age, and dried out again as the glaciers retreated. Rain now averages one inch yearly, and the last significant rainfall was in about 3400 BC, or a thousand years before the 4th Dynasty. Meanwhile, the nearby undisputed 4th Dynasty ruins show no such erosion—chisel marks are still visible. Mud-brick tombs from the days of the first pharaohs (who showed up in about 3100 BC) are also still around, and these would have dissolved in extended rain.

Consequently there are those who say the Sphinx must have been built before the pharaohs, and some push construction back as far as 7000 BC.

Meanwhile, modern mythology has gotten into the act, with mystic Edgar Cayce saying at several times in the 1930s and '40s that the records of Atlantis are preserved in a chamber in the bedrock in the vicinity of the Sphinx, implying that the Sphinx has prehistoric origins. So far, investigators have found only cracks in the rocks.

Assuming the Sphinx is prehistoric, and assuming it was not built by refugees from the sinking of Atlantis, we have to assume it was built by an indigenous culture that included people who could handle masonry construction, because the Sphinx is part masonry. But you don't see masonry in pre-pharaoh Egypt. Stone construction was limited to placing large stones to make monuments. For everyday purposes they relied on bricks made from plentiful mud. So we have to accept the idea that its builders finished the Sphinx and then went back to mud brick, attempting no further masonry construction for centuries.

Of course the people who built stonehenges, Aztec pyramids, German zeppelins, and Apollo moon rockets also all stopped doing so at some point. But we have other artifacts from these same cultures (especially the latter) that allow us to say with confidence that they did exist. (The same cannot be said about our friends from Atlantis.) If there was an otherwise unknown prehistoric culture in Egypt that built the Sphinx, it has not left a single pot or grave. Saying they must have existed because the Sphinx is there amounts to logic that's a little too circular for some. On the other hand, evidence of them could have washed away in whatever event eroded the Sphinx.

There is some middle ground among those who say that 4th Dynasty construction served to channel the existing rainfall runoff to the Sphinx, so it got all the erosion. So it was probably built before the 4th Dynasty, but during dynasties 1 through 3 rather than in pre-pharaoh Egypt.

At this point there seems to be no way to conclusively settle the matter. There may never be. The fact that the word *sphinx* is a synonym for enigma may not be a coincidence.

Except that, in actual fact, the association of the word *sphinx* with the Sphinx of Giza is pretty much of a coincidence. *Sphinx* comes from the Greek word for "strangle," and stems from the Greek legend (used as a plot device in Sophocles' 429 BC sellout play "Oedipus Rex") of an enigmatic monster with the head of a woman, the body of a lion, wings of an eagle, and tail of a snake. This generic sphinx haunted the roads outside the Greek city of Thebes, strangling (hence the name) and devouring anyone who could not answer its riddle: what creature walks on four legs in the morning, two at noon, and three in the evening? The hero (realizing that the time references are metaphorical) answers correctly: man, who walks on all fours as an infant, two legs as an adult, and three (with the use of a cane) in old age. The distraught monster then throws itself off the first available cliff, and the hero kills his own father and marries his own mother, living unhappily and fascinating Freudians ever after. The name stuck to the Egyptian mythological hybrid man-cat beast, as it was reminiscent of the sphinx, albeit simplified, lacking wings and the serpent tail.

Finally, there is one legend about the Sphinx of Giza that can be exploded with some certainly: that it lacks a nose because Napoleon's troops used it for artillery practice. A French army under Napoleon did invade Egypt in 1798 and was stranded there for three years after Napoleon's fleet was destroyed by the British. But the record indicates that they had more pressing things to do than fire scarce ammo at monuments. The record does indicate that the nose was chiseled off by a religious fanatic in 1378.

ARTIFACTS OUT OF TIME

One of the arguments in favor of the existence of flying saucers goes like this: Yes, a lot of reports of unidentified things in the sky turn out to be readily explained. But after discarding those reports you're left with things that cannot be explained, leaving open the possibility that there could be extraterrestrials hovering up there.

Of course, you could use the same argument in favor of the existence of elves—there must be, somewhere, reports of sightings that cannot be written off to insanity, drunkenness, or compulsive blathering. So the possibility remains that they could exist.

So let's apply the argument to the subject at hand: If the space-time continuum is a little soggy around the edges, you'd expect objects to show up that simply don't fit their settings, in terms of time, space, or both.

As this chapter demonstrates, that's the case.

As for elves, you'll be happy to know that in Iceland it's common to see roads re-routed and other construction projects altered to avoid disrupting the habitat of the local variety of elf (known as huldufólk.)

As for the flying saucers, don't press your luck.

11

The Voynich Manuscript

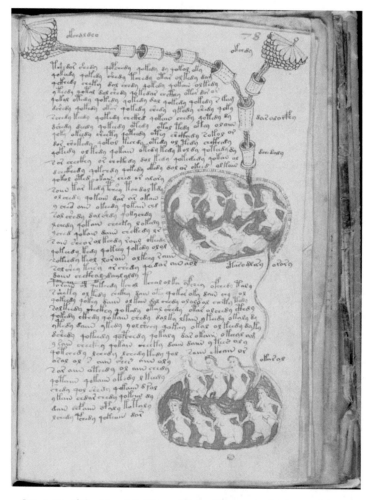

One page of the Voynich Manuscript, with text and images that continue to defy analysis. Public domain file from Wikimedia Commons.

It was laboriously produced by hand in about 1420, a generation before the printing press was introduced in Europe. It covers 240 pages of vellum (fine leather used as paper), although originally it may have been longer. It includes many illustrations, drawn by hand. The lettering was also done by hand, of course.

The existence and survival of this book, and countless others like it from the pre-Gutenberg era, is a testament to the fact that there are people who take learning seriously, and are willing to put major effort into the transmission of learning even in the absence of any mechanical aids—as was the case when the Middle Ages. Fortunately for the history of humanity, that's no mystery, as scholars down the centuries have demonstrated their commitment to the process.

But in the case of the Voynich Manuscript, there are serious mysteries. it is named after a New York book dealer who got his start after escaping from a Tsarist prison camp in Siberia and who acquired the manuscript in 1912. Modern analysis shows that it was indeed hand-produced in about 1420. But:

- The lettering employs an alphabet that is unknown outside this manuscript.
- The language that it uses appears to follow consistent rules and patterns, but they are the rules and patterns of no known language.
- Some of the illustrations appear to present botanical information about specific plants. They match no known plants.
- Some of the illustrations appear to present astronomical information. They match nothing known to astronomy.

So we have a manuscript whose production must have required months of sustained effort by a skilled artisan, and whose contents are organized as if they are supposed to make sense, but it's gibberish. Generations of scholars have refused to accept that possibility, and have subjected the manuscript to sustained cryptanalysis. These scholars have included some of the leading lights in the field of code-breaking.

The conclusion is that the text was written smoothly, as if by someone who knew the language, whatever it is. It uses an alphabet with several dozen letters—the exact number is debatable as the handwriting sometimes gets sloppy, and some letters may be variants of others. But about 30 letters are heavily used. The letters are divided into about 30,000 words. The words exhibit the kind of mathematical patterns you'd expect from a language rather than random doodles or psychotic word salad. Additionally, some words appear throughout the manuscript while others appear only in specific sections, as if they belong to the vocabulary of the subject in question.

As for the syntax, some words are repeated three times in a row, and others are repeated with only slightly different spellings. Some letters appear only at the start or the end of a word, and others only in the middle. (This is the case, for instance, with Arabic, but the text doesn't otherwise share any characteristics with Arabic.) There are letters that apparently act like vowels, as every word must have at least one such letter. Some letters never follow certain other letters. Some appear in doublets or triplets, and others never do.

Various decryptions and translations have been proposed, and all have been shot down. The text remains unreadable.

But even if the text could be read, the diagrams would still seem more than a little odd—and there is some kind of artwork on almost every page. The drawings include botanical diagrams of nonexistent plants, foldouts of what may be diagrams of unidentified celestial objects or magnified organic cells (or just elaborate doodles), and naked women in baths fed with elaborate, impractical plumbing—unclothed women in un-erotic poses is a recurring theme.

Basically, it cannot be proved that the manuscript contains any actual information that a third party could retrieve, despite closely emulating books that do exactly that. That being the case, surely it's:

- A hoax.
- Someone's expression of his or her obsessive-compulsive disorder.
- Something else.

Calling it a hoax solves the mystery of the manuscript's lack of decipherable meaning—but sets up a bigger mystery. Hoaxes are usually intended to make a quick buck, and not demonstrate the complexities of an invented language, or show how close the artist can come to representing something graphically while representing nothing. Even if the perpetrator did go to such lengths, you'd assume he'd eventually slip up and actually communicate something.

If the text were real material that had been encrypted for some reason, cryptanalysis should reveal the underlying "plain text." Some have suggested that the text was originally gibberish that was then encrypted in a way that caused it to take on the previously noted language-like mathematical patterns. That would account for the lack of meaning. But if it was a hoax the perpetrator was probably planning to dupe a book collector rather than the CIA. The CIA might be kept bemused a little longer with encrypted gibberish rather than raw gibberish when buying a book that was supposed to be in a foreign language, but the average book collector would not have been able to tell the difference.

As for the creation of the manuscript being an expression of OCD—well, a compulsion is a compulsion, but few OCD sufferers in the Middle Ages would have had access to the necessary tools and materials. Creating the manuscript for its own sake would have been a very expensive and unlikely hobby, but there were undoubtedly people in a position to do it—legitimate manuscripts that genuinely conveyed information were regularly being produced by somebody, after all. Maybe one of the people doing it was also an OCD sufferer. It would only take one.

But that assumes the perpetrator could have been able to construct a stand-alone language capable of filling a book while confounding modern analysis. There have been cases of people constructing their own languages, not to mention their own realities, and presumably there could have been such a person in the Middle Ages who additionally had the skills, material, and time to create something like the Voynich Manuscript. Would that same person also have had the time and skill to produce reams of artwork that were equally devoid of meaning? The combination seems unlikely.

That brings us to the possibility that there is something else going on. Consider this: If the manuscript is a hoax or an OCD artifact, the reason that we cannot understand the contents of the manuscript is because the subject matter existed only in the mind of the author. Therefore, we are not in touch with it and have no basis for understanding it. But the subject matter could also exist outside the mind of the author and we would still have no contact with it—because we have no connection with the context of the information. And that would be the case if it originated in some other place, or from some other time.

In the Introduction we considered the possibility of a reverse anachronism of the second kind—something from the future whose nature we are not equipped to appreciate. Typically, we assign it some alternate meaning (or assume that it has no meaning) until the time comes that we can appreciate its true meaning. If the Voynich manuscript is such an entity, and we cannot settle on an alternate meaning to assign to it (or assure ourselves that is has no meaning), then we are fated to remain mystified until its time comes.

Or, maybe someone harnessed his or her language and graphics-related compulsion for the purpose of duping a Middle Ages book collector.

12
Pharaonic Toy Airplane

The Saqqara Bird, found in an ancient Egyptian tomb, could be a very out-of-place toy airplane—or a bird figurine, or a weather vane. Wikimedia Commons image by Dawoudk. Used under license.

Toy airplanes. They line the shelves of toy stores and hobby shops. Some exist solely to model the appearance of real airplanes in exquisite detail; some are meant to fly, and their appearance is secondary; and some are meant to merely suggest the appearance of airplanes, while their main purpose is to be dragged around a sand box.

That's all well and good—but you don't expect to find one in an ancient Egyptian tomb.

And that brings us to the so-called Saqqara Bird, found in an Egyptian tomb in the Saqqara burial grounds (hence the name), south of modern Cairo, in 1898. Dated to about 200 BC, it is carved from cypress wood and has a 7-inch wing span. It resembles a top-wing monoplane except that the nose makes no provision for a cockpit window or a propeller, and the nose is shaped and decorated to resemble the head of a falcon.

The tail, however, is upright, and therefore resembles the tail of an airplane rather than a bird. There are neither feet nor landing gear. There is a mounting hole on the bottom at the center of gravity in line with the center of the wing, but that might be of modern origin. There are no representations of either feathers or control surfaces.

In other words, it is neither an entirely convincing airplane, nor an entirely convincing bird. It does seem to nicely match the description of a reverse anachronism, as laid out in the Introduction. Originally, it was a reverse anachronism from the future, as it was not recognized as an airplane when it was discovered in 1898, airplanes not having been invented yet. After airplanes with standard configurations (with a vertical stabilizer in the rear and a wing near the front) came into wide circulation it was recognized as a reverse anachronism from the then-present.

But such recognition presupposes that the object is actually intended to represent an airplane. Interpretations seem to be based on faith as much as anything else, and lead in three directions:

- It demonstrates that the Egyptians had knowledge of aerodynamics, and then lost that knowledge.
- It's a toy bird. Its resemblance to a modern airplane is accidental.
- It's a weather vane. Its resemblance to a modern airplane is accidental.

Addressing that first one—you'd think that if the ancient Egyptians had such knowledge it would be represented by more than one toy. Meanwhile, without lightweight engines, knowledge of aerodynamics would only allow them to make gliders and sailplanes, presumably launched through some combination of cliffs and drop-weights. With sufficient glide ratios they might be able to stay aloft for a while by catching updrafts and thermals. Doing so would offer important military reconnaissance advantages, which would not go unrecorded. But getting to that level would require detailed technical knowledge of a wide range of topics. (They would have to understand glide ratios, updrafts, and thermals, for starters.) Success would also have required step-by-step development, as perfecting techniques for getting airborne would then have to be followed by perfecting techniques for staying airborne (that is, flight control).

That's certainly the way it was done in the latter half of the 19th century, as multiple would-be aviation pioneers found that building wings and leaving the ground mostly resulted in traumatic landings—unless there was careful attention to the problems of flight control. Few tried it more than once. The first person to do so with any success was evidently German Otto Lilienthal, who made as many as 2,000 glides from 1891 until his death in a crash in 1896. Hoping to do better (not die) the Wright Brothers purposely approached the problem of flight from the control viewpoint, starting out with kites and moving on to gliders, adding power in late 1903.

In the ancient world you don't see much of that kind of purposeful, incremental research and development, if only because the lack of a publishing industry meant that one researcher could not readily build on the results of another. Indeed, secrecy, not openness, was the norm.

Meanwhile, if there was someone in ancient Egypt with enough foresight or foreknowledge to know that human flight was even possible, surely that person would concentrate on building a hot air balloon. He or she could get immediate, demonstrable results. The ability to station a lookout several hundred feet in the air for about 20 minutes on a relatively stable platform is something a pharaoh on campaign could have appreciated. The brief, uncertain results of launching a glider would have seemed laughable by comparison.

Finally, let's note that the tomb was dated to about 200 BC. The quality of historical documentation that survives from ancient times varies enormously, and the average from any random era is probably close to zero. Therefore, you can always say that a given event or technology could have slipped under the radar. But 200 BC puts us in the middle of the cataclysmic Punic Wars, which convulsed the Mediterranean basin for three generations. Historians were busy scribbling, and a great deal of their work survives, including lots of pure gossip. If someone in the region could fly during that era, we would surely have heard about it.

Meanwhile, if the Saqqara Bird was based on aeronautical knowledge, it did a poor job of representing it. Basically, it doesn't have a horizontal stabilizer—the small wing that's part of the tail. Without it, the Saqqara Bird—or any flying machine or glider that it was supposed to represent—could not fly, and would flop to the ground as soon as it was launched.

True believers insist that the horizontal stabilizer was omitted or lost (although there is no obvious place for one.) When a horizontal stabilizer is added to a reproduction of the artifact, it can be thrown so that it settles upright to the ground, with a glide ratio that's hardly worth mentioning.

Of course, maybe it was just a toy. But if the original owner wanted a throwing toy, he or she would have been happier with a boomerang (which the Egyptians had). If the Egyptians knew how to make toy gliders, they didn't bother to do so in this case.

Of course, plenty of modern toys are pretty miserable representations of real objects, especially the toys meant to be pushed through a sandbox. But 22 centuries from now there will probably be more evidence that we possessed airplanes than one airplane-like toy. There would be depictions and accounts of airplanes even if no individual airplanes survived, and of course there would be the remains of airports and related artifacts. Surely, there would be no mystery, and historians could confidently attest that aerodynamic knowledge became firmly established between the Roosevelt and Bush dynasties.

Meanwhile, if we're in a mood to assign whole technologies to the Egyptians on the basis of single, isolated objects or inscriptions, the fun never ends. There's a glyph in one temple inscription that looks like a side view of an Apache helicopter gunship. Experts say it's an illusion caused by later, heavy-handed editing. There's an inscription at another temple that some insist represents a neon light bulb. (Or the "bulb" could be snakes wrapped in a lotus blossom, both of which had religious meaning.) There are images in certain temple reliefs that—when the lighting is right—look just like popular representations of space aliens. (You can get similar effects without going all the way to Egypt, with clouds, or scraps of moldy bread.)

So the simplest explanation is that we are left with the second or third alternative, that it's a toy or a weather vane. Of course, if it's a toy bird, surely the tail would be flat. But a vertical tail is just right for a weather vane.

But on first glance it does look strikingly like an airplane.

13
Kennewick Man

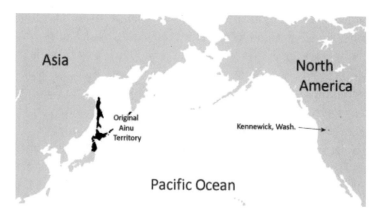

If Kennewick Man truly were a member of the Ainu people, this map shows that he was a long way from home. Map by the author.

The Americas were settled by people hiking in from the Old World, taking advantage of lower ocean levels during the last ice age that let them walk from Siberia to Alaska. The first tourists began showing up in Alaska about 15,000 years ago, and what is now the central United States had a stable population of natives (formerly called Indians) producing culturally distinct artifacts 13,500 years ago. Being from Asia they had Asiatic features, as do their descendents today. Aside from a brief Viking incursion about AD 1003 in Newfoundland, Europeans with their Caucasian genetics did not show up until AD 1492.

So far, so good. Then in 1996 the nearly complete skeleton of an unidentified Caucasian male in his 50s, standing 5-feet 8-inches high, was found in flooded bottomland in Kennewick, Washington. There was an arrowhead embedded in the right pelvis, but the bone had healed, indicating he had survived the attack. There were 19th century artifacts in the bottomland, so the deceased was assumed to be a forgotten pioneer. But when they looked closer at the embedded arrowhead, they saw it was not one of the types used in the region during the 19th century. To tell the truth, it resembled arrowheads that were known to be thousands of years old.

So they ran some tests on the skeleton. The conditions of the bones did not allow DNA testing, but carbon dating was possible. The results were unsettling.

It was 9,300 years old.

For a skeleton found in the Pacific Northwest, being Caucasian and 9,300 years old are supposed to be mutually exclusive attributes. Europeans showed up with their Caucasian features 500 years ago. Anyone getting shot with an arrow there and limping away 9,300 years ago ought to have had Asian features.

Of course, there have always been some who believe that Europeans using Eskimo technology could have made it to North America during the last ice age, following the edge of the ice pack. But then Kennewick Man, as he quickly became known, would have faced a long hike across the continent, crossing several mountain ranges before meeting his demise along the Columbia River.

This was a man absolutely out of place in both time and space.

The remains were then almost lost in a legal hall of mirrors, as various local Indian tribes laid claim to the skeleton. Sick of their ancestors' remains serving as curios, American Indian activists successfully pushed for passage of the Native American Graves Protection and Repatriation Act of 1990. It lets tribes take custody of any human remains to which they can reasonably assert cultural affinity, and inter them with their own rites.

Multiple tribes proceeded to assert custody over Kennewick Man. The initial test results indicated that their claim of kinship (reaching back about 465 generations) might be more than a little tenuous, but they persisted, and treated scientific examination as sacrilege. Battle lines were drawn, and the resulting vituperation was fully in keeping with long-standing academic traditions.

The bones were under the jurisdiction of the U.S. Army Corps of Engineers, having been found on land managed by the corps, and it responded to tribal pressure by retrieving the bones from the coroner and denying access to scientists. It even covered the discovery site with landfill and planted trees, lest additional bones be disturbed.

The scientists responded in a fashion fully in keeping with long-standing mainstream American traditions: interminable litigation. The scientists were finally upheld in 2004 when a federal court decided that the tribes had failed to show any cultural affinity, and scientists were allowed renewed access to the bones.

The results of further research indicate that the Indian activists need not have bothered, as the results upheld the world view or political agenda of nobody in particular. (Science can be annoying like that.) It turns out that although Kennewick Man had Caucasoid (that is, Caucasian-like) features, that does not make him a Caucasian. Giving differing weight to various factors, they decided that the Kennewick Man was more closely related to either of two modern populations:

- The Ainu of northern Japan.
- Nobody.

The Ainu were indigenous hunter-gatherers who were pushed into the northern part of Japan by the spread of the agricultural culture that became modern Japan. Their facial hair and light skin is reminiscent of Caucasian features, but DNA testing has shown no real link. But, given their location, it would be no surprise if ancestors of the Ainu took part in the migration to the Americas. Kennewick Man might be one result.

As for Nobody, there was no correlation to any modern population if the scientists disregarded size. It turns out that what few remains have surfaced in the Americas which are older than 8,000 years show considerable genetic diversity. These include Luiza, the skull of a woman found in Brazil in 1975, thought to be 11,500 years. Her features were distinctly African.

There's also the Buhl Woman, a skull found in a quarry in Idaho in 1989, and found to be 10,675 years old. Her features were reminiscent of Polynesians. Despite this, the bones were soon turned over to local Indians for reburial under the previously mentioned Native American Graves Protection and Repatriation Act.

This does not mean that prehistoric Japan, Tahiti, and Africa were in regular contact with the Americas. It does indicate that people carrying genes from populations that settled in those locations also showed up in the Americas—and that prehistoric migrations were more complex than we currently understand. Homo sapiens sapiens (that's us) have been around for 200,000 years, leaving plenty of time for wandering around and inter-marrying, a process still under way. Presumably, the diversity represented by the Kennewick, Buhl, and Luiza remains was washed out by later migrations.

Deciding what it all truly means must wait until a lot more evidence surfaces. In that sense Kennewick Man is truly a reverse anachronism from the future, assuming that there will come a time when we can confidently trace ancient migrations and the process by which humanity settled Planet Earth. In the meantime we must accept our ignorance.

Oddly, facial forensic reconstruction of the Kennewick Man's skull produced a bust that looked remarkably like British actor Patrick Stewart, best known for starring in the *Star Trek: The Next Generation* science-fiction TV series about interstellar space exploration. The resemblance is doubtless accentuated by the actor's and the bust's shared lack of hair.

Kennewick Trek? Well, at some point in the settling of the Earth, someone had to boldly go where no person had gone before. Hollywood can't beat the real story.

14
Really Lost Penny

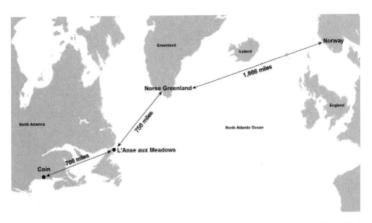

A coin minted in Norway by the son of the Viking leader who died trying to invade England in 1066 somehow ended up in the rubbish pit of an Indian village in what is now Maine. As this map shows, it did some serious traveling. Map by the author.

Coins can show up in odd places, and the record may have been set by the so-called Maine Penny. It was found five feet underground in 1957 during an excavation of the rubbish mound of an ancient American Indian village near Blue Hill, Maine. Further excavations uncovered no other similar artifacts at the site.

It was silver and about the size of a dime. One side showed a cross inside a circle, while the other showed the stylized head of some animal, perhaps a rooster or even a dragon.

So far, so good—until they finally figured out where it came from. Coins like that were made in Norway during the early years of the reign of Olaf the Peaceful (he never started any wars), who was king of Norway from 1067 to 1093. And that presents problems of space and time.

As for space, Blue Hill is centrally located on the coast of Maine, about 3,300 miles from Norway, and there were never any Norse settlements in Maine. Of course, the Norse are known to have founded a village on the northern tip of Newfoundland, at a place now called L'Anse aux Meadows. That's "only" a thousand miles away from Blue Hill. The inhabitants are known to have made forays further south, due to the presence in their rubbish of butternuts, which prefer warmer weather and don't grow in Newfoundland.

But that brings us to the problem of time, as L'Anse aux Meadows was set up in about AD 1000 and abandoned within 10 years—it did not even have a cemetery, for instance. So it was forgotten by the time Olaf the Peaceful was even born.

Of course, the people at L'Anse aux Meadows were from the group of Norse (also called Viking) pioneers who set up a colony in Greenland in 985, resettling from Iceland. That colony started out with only 14 boat-loads of people, so there was probably no pressing need for expansion 15 years later. But the Greenland colony survived for another 400 years and at one point consisted of about 600 farms and several thousand people. There would have been plenty of opportunity for contact with the Indians on the mainland of North America, if only because the Greenlanders would have wanted to go there for lumber. (Greenland, to put it mildly, is not heavily forested.)

So if we assume the penny arrived through Greenland after the coronation of Olaf the Peaceful in 1067, we are trading space for time, as Greenland is 1,500 miles from Blue Hill. Of course, those Norse Greenlanders had ocean-going boats, and could get around. In fact, Norse artifacts have shown up all over the eastern Canadian arctic, indicating that the Norsemen traded extensively with the natives—as you'd expect. The Norse economy was based primarily on maritime trade, and they had trading networks stretching to the Caspian Sea. Raiding was a sideline, although it got a lot more attention then and still does now.

That being the case, you'd think there would be plenty of Norse artifacts in or involving the United States. But aside from the Maine Penny, there are only three that anyone has ever pointed to:

1. The Kensington Stone, a slab with a Norse rune inscription that turned up on a farm in Minnesota in 1898. The inscription tells of casualties among a Norse exploring party in 1362.

2. The Newport Tower in Newport, Rhode Island, which looks like a round fortification tower of rough masonry, 28 feet tall. There is no record of its construction.

3. Yale University's Vinland Map, a map of the world made before Columbus that appears to show Greenland and part of North America, labeled Vinland, implying extensive Norse exploration efforts.

But the Maine Penny differs from these three in one important aspect: It's considered genuine, and the other three are considered bogus. The Kensington Stone and the Vinland map are now considered hoaxes, and the Newport Tower appears to have been a derelict windmill, originally used for grinding meal, and built about 1675. So, aside from the Maine Penny, no other genuine Norse artifacts have been found in the United States.

So the Vikings left graffiti in Constantinople, a colony in Greenland, a village in Newfoundland, but only one penny in Maine, and nothing in the rest of the United States. Apparently, the bulk of North America offered nothing that they wanted.

That seems odd, considering the mad dash that the Spanish, Portuguese, and other Europeans made to the New World as soon as it was discovered. The simplest explanation is that, despite their fearsome Viking reputation, the Norsemen truly were traders at heart, and commuted to North America strictly for business. Presumably, this meant profitably supplying Europeans with things they could only get along the fringes of the arctic, especially ivory from tusks. Presumably, after the Crusades ended it was easier to get ivory out of Africa, profits ebbed, and the Norse Greenlanders looked for opportunities elsewhere.

The last recorded Norse event in Greenland was a wedding in 1408, followed by the couple's relocation to Iceland. Today's archeologists find very little in Greenland's surviving Norse ruins, as if the previous residents packed carefully.

But before they packed up, they had four centuries of interaction with the natives. Trade must have been through barter, as the Indians and Eskimos did not have a monetary economy. Coins would have bartered as decorative items or curios, and presumably natives passed them from hand to hand into regions far removed from those that were actually in contact with the Norsemen. One penny ended up in Blue Hill.

In other words, in all likelihood the coin did not fall out of the pocket of some member of a very lost Viking raiding party. The coin's maker, Olaf the Peaceful, would have been happy to hear that, having himself given up on war in favor of trade and diplomacy. As a teenage prince he accompanied his father, King Harald Hardrada, during the Norwegian invasion of England in 1066, in a war triggered by a disagreement over who should succeed the late English King Edward the Confessor.

The Norwegian armada of 300 ships landed in the Yorkshire area of northeast England. Olaf was offshore in one of the ships when the defending English

King Harold Godwinson unexpectedly arrived with a large army and launched a stunningly successful surprise attack, killing Olaf's father and quite a few other Norsemen. (In the pre-fight parlay Godwinson offered Hardrada just enough English land for a grave. Hardrada declined, and was indeed later buried in Norway.) Olaf managed to organize a truce and withdraw.

The English king survived another three weeks, dying at the Battle of Hastings while trying unsuccessfully to repel yet another invasion, this one by Duke William of Normandy. The result is known as the Norman Conquest and is one reason why so many French words show up in English.

As for Olaf the Peaceful, he was eventually succeeded by Magnus the Barefoot, who, despite the name (or because of it) immediately launched a career of insatiable conquest. The resulting campaigns are considered the swansong of the Viking era. He died in battle in 1103 while attempting to conquer Ireland.

Meanwhile, the Norse identity of the Maine Penny was not confirmed until 1979. (It was originally assumed to be a Renaissance British coin, which would have been easier to explain.) Ironically, that was two years after the publication of *Runestruck*, a comic novel by Calvin Trillin about a small town on the coast of Maine being thrown into chaos after locals find a Norse artifact on the beach. In the novel the artifact is a stone covered with runes rather than a coin. More importantly, in the real world the reaction was subdued rather than frenzied.

Perhaps the real Maine villagers had read Trillian's book and knew how not to act. Or maybe Olaf was looking out for them.

PRACTICES, BELIEFS, AND KNOWLEDGE

There are words for a professional who does not use the latest advances and discoveries in his or her field. "Incompetent" is probably the least harsh of them.

But what about someone who uses those advances or discoveries before they are made?

There appears to be no word for that. But as the examples in this section show, there are genuine, documented cases. Some of them beat the gun by centuries. There is also a case in which the possession of the knowledge was apparently an illusion, and another in which they were clearly guessing, albeit correctly.

In most cases the possessors of the foreknowledge got some benefit out of it—otherwise we probably would not have heard about it. But it also appears that a positive outcome was not guaranteed. Apparently, "success" (whatever the word means in a particular situation) does not automatically result from having information that others lack.

But it's still handy, as you'll see.

Meanwhile, the question remains as to how they acquired their apparent foreknowledge. Read on, and you'll see that there is no simple answer.

15
Prince Hal's Modern Surgery

King Henry V, showing no disfigurement from the strangely modern facial surgery he underwent as a teenager. Public domain file from Wikimedia Commons.

Antiseptic surgery traces its roots to an 1867 article titled "Antiseptic Principle of the Practice of Surgery" in a British medical journal by Dr. Joseph Lister, describing how he got remarkable results by sterilizing wounds and medical equipment with phenol, a.k.a. carbolic acid, a derivative of coal tar.

Before that, any kind of surgery was an extreme form of first aid, resorted to in desperation. Thanks to the risk of infection, the surgery itself was likely to be as dangerous as whatever condition was being treated.

So it's a little startling to see antiseptic surgery, with an additional item of seemingly modern surgical equipment, being performed in 1403.

In that year 16-year-old Henry of Monmouth was hit in the face by an arrow during the Battle of Shrewsbury in west-central England, as a member of the English army that was suppressing a local rebellion. A lot of other guys got shot with arrows that day, but young Henry was also the Prince of Wales and heir to the throne of England, and so received a level of attention that probably made the difference between life and death.

He was wearing his helmet but had left his visor up. Perhaps, like a modern tank commander, he was trying to maintain maximum visibility until the shooting started. When it did start he was immediately hit in the left side of the face, by the nose and below the eye. War arrowheads were heavy, sharp, and nasty, and were attached to the arrow shaft by jamming it into a socket at the bottom of the arrowhead. They were often held on with only a small amount of wax. Consequently, someone trying to pull it out of a victim would only manage to pull out the arrow shaft, leaving the arrowhead in the victim's flesh, where it would trigger a dangerous infection.

And that is what happened to Prince Henry. The arrow penetrated about six inches—any deeper would probably have been fatal. He was evacuated to a castle where various doctors tried to remove the arrowhead, without success. Finally they sent for John Bradmore, a royal retainer and London surgeon. Perhaps more importantly, he was also a goldsmith, making him familiar with the construction of small, intricate metal objects.

First, he opened the wound (presumably swollen shut) with wooden probes that had been infused with honey. He used larger and larger probes until the wound was as wide and deep as needed.

Then he used his skills as a goldsmith to make what we would call an extractor. Other arrow extractors that have come down to us were little more than metal rods that the surgeon jammed into the socket of the arrowhead, where he hoped it would stick long enough to be pulled out. Given the delicate placement of this arrowhead, that approach (invariably involving pushing the arrowhead in farther) would have been fatal.

So Bradmore put together, from scratch, a zero-force insertion tool with an adjustable-force grip. Think of a sugar tong, the two arms of which you pinch together so that their ends will grip a sugar cube. He made the arms of his tong long and narrow and cylindrical, so they could reach into the wound and fit into the socket of the arrowhead. Then, at the handle end of the tong he punched a hole through which he screwed a threaded rod.

When the time came to operate he inserted the ends of the tong arms into the exposed arrow socket. (He apparently had to do this by feel.) Then he screwed the rod down between the arms of the tong and into the arrowhead socket, where it spread the arms of the tong out against the inside of the socket. That gave him a firm grip on the arrowhead, which he slowly, carefully extracted.

He then washed the wound with wine and packed it with material that had been treated with honey and turpentine. He used less and less packing until (after about 20 days) the wound closed. Bradmore also kept giving his patient muscle-relaxing ointments and anti-spasm hot plasters, apparently to counter any tetanus symptoms.

Subsequent likenesses of Prince Henry (later King Henry V of England) show no facial disfigurement. He inherited the throne in 1413 and reigned until his death by disease while campaigning in France in 1422. He is chiefly remembered for crushing a French army at Agincourt in 1415, and for being a character in three plays of Shakespeare: Prince Hal in *Henry IV Part 1* and *Henry V Part 2*, and the title character in *Henry V*.

The mystery is Bradmore—how did he know to use honey, alcohol, and turpentine, which we know to have antibacterial properties? Almost anything else would have been fatal. But no one, including Bradmore (assuming he was not a time traveler) knew germs even existed until 1676.

Sometime before his death in 1412 he wrote a treatise that described what he did for the prince but it did not explain *why* he did what he did. That's probably because he was writing for an audience of fellow medieval surgeons who shared the same accumulated empirical knowledge, based on hard experience. They would have known that the Greeks and Romans had used wine and honey for wound treatment. Turpentine may have been a more recent discovery. Bradmore's extractor, however, must have been original to him.

Had Bradmore actually known about germs, he would have additionally heated his probe in a brazier just before use, something the Romans had learned to do with all surgical instruments. Or maybe he did heat it, and the act was too commonplace to mention. On the other hand, if he was a time traveler who knew about germs he would probably have felt helpless in the face of tetanus, knowing that the fatality rate without modern medicine is about 50 percent.

He never mentions the use of painkillers. Hopefully, that also was too commonplace to mention.

Finally, if you're shot with an arrow today, the surgeon will use aseptic rather than antiseptic methods—keeping germs away rather than killing them with acid. Among other things, the surgeon will scrub his or her hands and arms up to the elbow for several minutes before proceeding, in a sink with an effectively endless supply of hot running water.

And that's something Bradford probably could not have imagined.

16
Obviously Not Flat

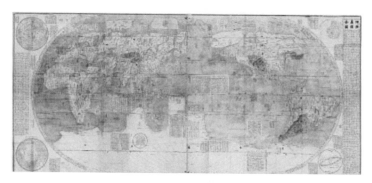

Although this map was made in China in 1602 it was not only surprisingly accurate, but used a map projection that was invented in 1906. Public domain image from Wikimedia Commons.

The world is round. The problem is that maps are flat. You can't depict the outlines of the world's surface features on a flat piece of paper without introducing massive distortions. There are multiple ways of approaching the problem, called projections, but they all involve tradeoffs.

One popular one has been used by National Geographic is the Eckert IV projection. It preserves equal areas so that, for instance, Greenland is not bigger than Africa. It was developed in 1906 by German geographer Max Eckert-Greifendorff.

And that's odd because it appears to have been used for the "Kunyu Wanguo Quantu," or "Map of the Myriad Countries of the World," a map of the world printed in China in 1602.

Better yet, the use of a modern map projection is by no means the only odd thing about this map. It is the oldest map made in China that shows the Americas. At first glance it appears to be accurate, which is hard to square with the inward-looking traditions of the Middle Kingdom at that time. Altogether it has so many odd features that cartographers call it The Impossible Black Tulip. (Clue: There are no black tulip flowers.)

First, let's talk about map projections. The generic one is the Mercator projection, in which the world is treated as a cylinder and basically rolled onto the flat map. The direction between any two points on the map is accurate, and navigators like that. But the areas of the landforms are increasingly distorted in the east-west direction as you get farther north or south of the equator, with the distortion becoming infinite at the poles. And so generations of schoolchildren got odd ideas about what country was bigger than what other country—especially about Greenland being larger than anything.

Because not everyone is a navigator, geographers have experimented with other approaches that modify the Earth-as-cylinder concept and strive for shape or size accuracy at the expense of directional accuracy. These are called pseudo-cylindrical projections. With the Eckert IV projection only the center meridian (the longitude or north-south lines) is a straight line. The rest of the meridians are increasingly curved as you get farther from the center, until the framing ones at either end of the map are semicircles. The east-west parallel or latitude lines are straight, but are not set at equal distances, getting closer together as they approach the poles. The central meridian, and the top and bottom pole lines, are half the length of the equator. Areas are accurate, but shapes and directions are distorted by varying amounts depending on how far away a point is from the central meridian at either 40.5 degrees north or south. At those two points things are perfect.

And that is (more or less) what we see with the Kunyu (as we'll call it), which was made 304 years before the Eckert IV was invented. The framing meridians at either ends are indeed semicircles, becoming less curved toward the central meridian, which is a straight vertical line. The central meridian is indeed half the length of the equator. Greenland is not the dominant landmass—in fact, the continents seem to have the correct proportional sizes.

In fact, all the continents except Australia are there, and their outlines are at least vaguely correct, down to the delineation of Baja California. Considering the map was made in China in 1602, and the Chinese were not then in the business of dispatching voyages of discovery, how could that be? Excited promoters of the paranormal are doubtless rushing to their blogs to announce the discovery of evidence of UFOs passing geographical information to the Ming Dynasty Chinese government, selectively misquoting the first half of this sentence as support.

On closer examination there is less of a mystery. There are three reasons for sticking to purely rational explanations for the Black Tulip. (Clue: There are no black tulips, but there are dark purple tulips that look black in the right lighting conditions.)

The first reason is that the map is known (from credits listed on it, for one) to be a product of Chinese geographers, using their local knowledge, in partnership with Matteo Ricci (1552 to 1610), a Jesuit missionary and trained scientist and cartographer from Italy. Ricci made special efforts to learn the Chinese language and culture, and (after he successfully predicted a solar eclipse) ended up being the first Westerner to be invited inside the Forbidden City. He was summoned there by the Ming emperor Wanli, but ended up never actually seeing the man. In fact, Wanli would spend the last 20 years of his life refusing to see his ministers, read any reports, or make any appointments, inaugurating an era of epic mismanagement that would eventually bring down the Ming Dynasty. But before he got fed up with politics and government he did ask Ricci to make him a world map. Ricci had made a point of keeping a world map on his wall to intrigue his Chinese guests, but it was annotated in the Roman alphabet and China was off to one side. The resulting custom map was annotated in Chinese and the Middle Kingdom was closer to the middle (although the central meridian was in the Pacific about where the Date Line is today). Ricci reportedly moved China closer to the middle less in an effort to massage the emperor's ego than to show the Chinese how far away Europe was. The result is that European intruders like himself seemed less threatening.

The second reason that we can rely on rationality is that, on closer inspection, the map is not all that accurate. Europeans had been making world maps with increasing accuracy since 1507, based on the results of various voyages of discovery and expanded trade routes, but the results were not all in by 1602. If the map's makers had access to some mysterious source of information, Australia and New Guinea would not be part of Antarctica, the Caspian Sea would not be rotated 90 degrees, Hudson Bay would be bigger and not drained by the St. Lawrence Seaway, the islands of Indonesia would line up correctly, and the Pacific Ocean would not be speckled with large, random islands.

The third reason is that it is possible that the map-makers were not actually using the Eckert IV projection. The pole line is not quite half the length of the equator, as required by Eckert IV (although it's hard to measure.) Also, the latitude lines should get closer together as they approach the poles, and on the Kunyu they don't seem to do that. Admittedly, the map-makers could have been aiming for such a projection, having invented it themselves, but were not able to achieve the necessary precision. But it's just as likely that they simply wanted a layout that left room in the corners of the map to include extra information, much as National Geographic does today with its world maps. In the end they came up with something that resembles the Eckert IV projection. On the left side there is a north polar view in the top corner and a south polar view in the bottom corner. The right corners contain astronomical information with a geocentric layout. There would be no available corners if they had used a standard, rectangular Mercator projection.

The resulting map was a black-and-white woodblock print on six rolls of paper, altogether 12.5 feet wide and 5.5 feet high, and was intended to be displayed on a folding screen. About a thousand copies were made, of which six survive. Copies in local languages quickly appeared in Japan and in Korea, and smaller, color copies proliferated in which the oceans were blue and seemingly random territories were green, pink, and yellow.

We can't call this one a reverse anachronism of any sort, because it was firmly rooted in its time. We can't call it a bleeding-edge phenomenon because no suffering resulted. We can say that its creators made the best possible use of the available resources. Sadly, that's rare. In this case the results leap to our attention because they seem startlingly modern—a black tulip, indeed.

17
Archimedes, Now and Forever

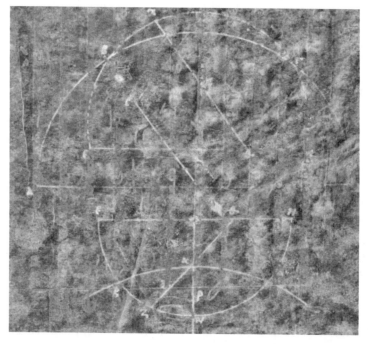

Partially recovered diagram of a geometrical proof found on the previously erased pages of the last surviving manuscript copy of the works of Archimedes. Archimedes Palimpsest data is released with license for use under Creative Commons Attribution 3.0 Unported Access Rights.

Terrifying machines that are starkly out of time, and death rays—for most geniuses, these would be enough for one career. But when it comes to reverse anachronisms, Archimedes was just getting started.

As detailed previously, Archimedes repelled a Roman army in 214 BC with machines that induced panic in the beholders—and seem astonishingly modern today.

But when you examine some of his writings you start to seriously worry about who was playing with the time machine.

Archimedes left a number of propositions and treatises, totaling about 100,000 words. (That's the equivalent of a moderately thick dime-store novel.)

He did not mention military machines in his writing, and that silence was probably intentional.

He did write quite a bit about determining the volume of curved shapes. Ships' hulls, you'll note, have a lot of curves. Once you determine their volume, you can determine their weight, and then calculate what force it would take to spoil their day. And that is what his machines did, when the Romans attacked Syracuse, as previously described.

When designing such anti-ship machines it also would help if you were an expert on equilibrium, buoyancy, and the behavior of floating bodies. As it happens, Archimedes wrote a two-volume treatise on that topic.

Developing methods for finding the center of gravity for various shapes would also be helpful. As you were probably about to guess, he wrote a lot about that, too.

Meanwhile, the appreciation—in fact, the survival—of his writings provide a textbook case of a reverse anachronism of the second kind graduating to the first kind.

Aside from some that have surfaced from ancient Egyptian garbage dumps, where the desert preserved them, ancient Greek and Roman writings survive to the present only because enough people throughtout the centuries considered them worth the effort of copying and recopying. Typically they started life on papyrus scrolls, and as those decayed in late antiquity the material was copied to parchment codexes (hand-bound sheepskin books). What we have today are typically second-generation copies of those parchment codexes, made during the Dark Ages.

Archimedes barely made the cut. Only three manuscripts with overlapping selections of his works in the original Doric Greek survived the Dark Ages. This lack of popularity may be because the contents were so far over the heads of its readers.

Two of the codexes were lost in the Renaissance and survive only through translations in other languages. The third surfaced again in 1874, was subject to some study, and then dropped out of sight—until 1999, when a dot-com billionaire (Jeff Bezos) acquired it and gave it to a museum in Baltimore for study.

This codex was a palimpsest, meaning that someone had taken the original manuscript, erased Archimedes' writing, rebound it, and reused it, in this case as a prayer book. But some of the erased material was still visible, and had been partially transcribed in 1906. Using modern imaging, researches set about making much more of it visible—and found material that no one had read for centuries. They were also able to make better sense out of some of the previously known material.

The results were humbling. They found Archimedes demonstrating an understanding of the concept of infinite summation. This is the basis of calculus, normally traced back no earlier than Isaac Newton in 1671.

Archimedes also demonstrated an understanding of the need to avoid the paradoxes that can arise when dealing with infinite quantities: Assume that A equals infinity. Let B equal two times A. Therefore B is also equal to infinity. But infinity equals infinity. Therefore B equals A. Yet B is two times A... Avoiding such paradoxes is the basis of set theory, which originated in the 1870s.

So his writings have been around for more than 2,200 years, but only within the last 150 years had they fully transformed into a reverse anachronism of the first kind.

As for an explanation, apparently his intellect sufficed to invent what he needed to achieve his goals, which involved constructing huge machines from first principles. Perhaps we can compare him to Newton who likewise invented what he needed (calculus) to achieve his goals, which involved finding an explanation for orbital motion.

Meanwhile, some of the erased text on the last Archimedes manuscripts remains unreadable, or (if we're lucky) scattered unrecognized in other palimpsested prayer books from the Middle Ages. Who knows, Archimedes may still have a reverse anachronism of the second kind out there, awaiting our ability to comprehend it.

18
The Nelson (Future) Touch

*Admiral Nelson, who appears to have won the decisive Battle of
Trafalgar with plans based on a method of mathematical analysis
that was not invented for another century. Public domain image
from Wikimedia Commons.*

They're called the Lanchester Equations, or the N-Squared Law of Mutual
Attrition. They mathematically describe how military forces inflict casual-
ties on each other, and were published in 1916 by English engineer Frederick
Lanchester in a pioneering treatise about aerial combat.

They also appear to have been used by Admiral Lord Nelson in drawing up plans for the wildly successful Battle of Trafalgar, the decisive naval battle of the Napoleonic Wars. Inconveniently, that was in 1805, 111 years before Lanchester's laws were published.

They called Nelson's management style "The Nelson Touch." The question is: What was he in touch with?

Lanchester's equations imply that the ratio between two forces with long-range weapons is based not on their numbers, but on the square of their numbers. For example, the superiority of force A with 5,000 facing force B with 4,000 is not a marginal 5 to 4, but a daunting 25 to 16. If A and B fight to a finish (which rarely happens in reality), B will be annihilated while A will lose 2,000 members, because the number of survivors for A (3,000) is defined as the square root of what's left when you subtract B squared from A squared. The equations show that even the smallest advantage can lead to eventual victory thanks to a snowballing effect that favors the superior force—but its members will need an overriding faith in victory to get them through the ensuing bloodbath. The smaller force also has to stand fast until annihilated, which is rare.

The equations have been used by military planners, wargame designers, and, yes, Japanese business consultants. But they need careful modification before they can be applied to real-world situations, primarily because they assume that both sides are equally exposed to each other's firepower. That's rarely the case. In infantry fighting, for instance, the defenders are usually behind cover while the attackers are moving through the open, which means there is no mutual exposure. But mutual exposure was the case, more or less, for naval warfare in the Age of Napoleon, when tall sailing ships-of-the-line with rows of muzzle-loading cannon traded broadsides in plain sight of each other.

That brings us to 1805, when a British fleet under Nelson had bottled up one of Napoleon's fleets in the harbor of Cadiz, Spain, as part of an ongoing effort to prevent Napoleon from invading England. The latest information was that the Napoleon had 46 ships-of-the-line in Cadiz while Nelson had 40 waiting outside Cadiz. According to Lanchester's laws, a battle would have led to the destruction of the British fleet, while leaving Napoleon's fleet with 23 ships—easily enough to mount an unopposed invasion.

It didn't work out that way. While he waited for the enemy to come out, Nelson made other plans. These were preserved in a written memo to his captains—being precedent-breaking, they required careful exposition.

Pre-modern sail-powered fleets usually maneuvered in a single-file follow-the-leader fashion that facilitated command control. Two fleets that wanted to fight would sail parallel to each other, closing to gun range and sparking a melee of ship-to-ship actions of the kind that movie-makers love. However, the loser could break off and retreat at any time.

Nelson would have none of that. He proposed approaching the enemy on a perpendicular rather than a parallel course, in three columns rather than one, moving directly for the center of the enemy battle line. The first column would have only eight ships. It would strike the enemy line a few ships ahead of the center. The second column with 16 ships would attack the enemy line right at its center. The third column, also with 16 ships, would attack the enemy line 12 ships from the rear.

Nelson did not explain why he was being so picky about where he wanted to attack the enemy line (at least not on paper). But it all became clear 111 years later.

If you stand back and admire the big picture, you see that, after Nelson's three-pronged maneuver, 23 ships at the rear of the enemy fleet would be facing 32 British ships. Lanchester's equations show that the British advantage in this melee was not 3 to 2, but actually 2 to 1. If they fought to a finish, the enemy rear would be annihilated while the British would lose 10 ships.

If the 23 ships in the front half of the enemy fleet tried to reverse course (a slow process for a sailing force) and reinforce the rear, they would first have to get through Nelson's eight-ship delaying force. According to the equations, they would defeat it, and lose two ships in the process. In the unlikely event that they pressed on, the 21 surviving enemy ships would then face the 22 surviving British ships in the rear. When the smoke cleared, the equations state that the British should still have seven ships, and Napoleon none—and that is a long way from the original setup, which left Napoleon with 23 and the British none.

In other words, the plan was perfect—according to mathematical rules discovered more than a century after Nelson's death.

When the day came (October 21, 1805), Napoleon's fleet emerged from Cadiz with 33 ships while the British were down to 27. The wind was light so Nelson dispensed with the eight-ship delaying force. His other two columns broke the enemy line a little ahead of the center, and the ships in the front of the enemy line proved uninterested in turning back to help. When the smoke cleared the British had captured 22 ships while losing none themselves. (According to the equations, the British should have lost eight while taking 22. But in practice, as Napoleon's fleet disintegrated, British ships that were in trouble could get backup.) Napoleon would never threaten England on the sea again. In fact, no power would do so until Lanchester's lifetime, and the British prevailed then, too.

This would appear to be a prime example of a reverse anachronism of the second kind (that is, from the future). Historians and commentators had no idea why Nelson's battle plan cited the numbers it did until 1916. Then the fog cleared, and his plan became a reverse anachronism of the first kind.

As for a simple explanation for Nelson's apparent foreknowledge, there isn't any. Presumably, he put a lot of effort into the problem of defeating the French fleet, and sought the best advice he could find—and the result resembled the N-Squared Law. He probably treated his methods as a military secret, and they died with him at Trafalgar, where he was killed by a French sniper.

Any time traveler with genuine foreknowledge of the equations would also have known about the realities of naval life in the era—wretched food, bad water; crowded, wet living conditions; crude navigation; an erratic power source; barbaric discipline; and the many inconveniences caused by incoming cannon balls—and would surely have remembered an urgent appointment elsewhere. Giving the entire credit to Nelson seems unavoidable.

19
Hurricane Pam

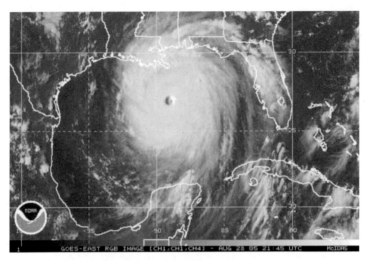

Hurricane Pam, had it ever existed, would doubtless have looked from space like this satellite image of Hurricane Katrina, which Hurricane Pam prophesized in great detail. NOAA image.

The hurricane came roaring towards New Orleans from the south in the early hours of September 26, 2004, and by the morning of the 28th the flooding had begun, rising to catastrophic levels by nightfall—after all, parts of the city are 20 feet below sea level. Thousands who had not heeded the call to evacuate were stranded in a flooded, ruined cityscape devoid of any services. The authorities resorted to "lily pad" tactics, moving the survivors in random batches, first to dry land, and then high ground, and finally to organized shelters.

Yes, Hurricane Katrina was bad news—except that the previous paragraph is not about Hurricane Katrina, which took place in late August 2005, wrecking the lives of countless residents of the U.S. Gulf Coast, and ending the credibility and/or careers of any number of politicians and bureaucrats.

Instead, we're talking about Hurricane Pam, which was the fictional creation of a five-day emergency preparedness wargame held in Baton Rouge in July 2004. It involved about 300 local officials and ought to have boosted their credibility and careers, as it unknowingly presented an almost hour-by-hour prophecy of what they would face 13 months later.

Glancing at a Pam-Katrina comparisons, you have to wonder who was playing with the time machine:

	Pam	Katrina
Rainfall	20 inches	18 inches
Wind	120 miles per hour	About 120 miles per hour at landfall in Louisiana
Pumping New Orleans dry	30 days	43 days
Displaced refugees	1 million from Louisiana	1 million from the Gulf Coast, predominant Louisiana
Evacuation rate	35 percent	80 percent plus
Number requiring medical help	About 175,000 injured, 200,000 ill	About 60,000 were treated
Fatalities	Not stated publicly, but apparently 10,000	At least 1,836
Buildings destroyed	500,000 to 600,000	About that, with 200,000 homes in New Orleans alone
Security situation	Not addressed	A debacle
Communications	Not addressed	Complete breakdown
Temporary houses needed for displaced persons	200,000	700,000 received some kind of housing assistance
Shelter capacity	Local resources could last three to five days and then they'd need outside help	No one seems to have read that memo
Lily pad tactics	Useful	Better than nothing

The big difference between the two scenarios is that the Pam planners assumed that only 35 percent of the population would evacuate. In fact, the rate was at least 80 percent with Katrina, resulting in far fewer casualties than the Pam projection. Beyond that, there seemed to be an unstated assumption with

Pam that the authorities could exert control where and as needed—that the government would remain functioning while all other social institutions were paralyzed by circumstances. Consequently, people who needed help could expect to get it, and lawlessness and looting would not be an issue. But of course 300 bureaucrats and officials weren't going to hold a wargame to explore the depths of their impotence—the participants had to be given something to do beyond wringing their hands.

But aside from the cheery absence of social chaos, official impotence, horrifying media images, and political scapegoating, Hurricane Pam was unrelentingly prophetic. Nevertheless, no psychic foreknowledge was claimed by or for the organizers, and no such power needs to be invoked to explain Pam. Obviously, the organizers were seeking a situation that would require the maximum resources from the maximum number of governmental and nonprofit agencies—to test them to destruction, so to speak. After all, anything less would not be as educational, and would certainly not justify getting 300 people together for a week. So the organizers cooked up a worst-case but realistic scenario, with a slow-moving Category 3 storm that would over-top the levees and flood New Orleans, not to mention numerous outlying areas.

By chance, Mother Nature appears to have had the same goal, and launched her version before all the planned Hurricane Pam follow-up conferences were completed. She did test them to destruction. The results were educational.

As for anyone citing the wargame later, after Katrina, and the supply of insights that made things easier—forget it. There was a chorus of apologists saying that the scale of the catastrophe was beyond anyone's foresight. President Bush said on TV that no one foresaw the breaching of the levees that flooded New Orleans, while the secretary of Home Security said that Katrina presented circumstances that were unforeseen. But as we've seen, Pam had almost everything that Katrina had, with even greater casualties.

Even without Hurricane Pam, there was no grounds for anyone to claim surprise. Ground level in New Orleans had been sinking below sea level for decades, and the outlying barrier islands that functioned as storm breaks had been eroding for decades. Every summer, at the start of hurricane season, the authorities would issue another set of warnings pointing out the dire situation that New Orleans would be in if this was the year of the Big One. The media would dutifully print them, with artful enhancements. But the city had not taken a direct hit from a major storm since Hurricane Betsy in 1965, which triggered serious flooding. There had been several evacuations since then in the face of approaching storms, but those storms had either veered to one side or fizzled out. In other words, the locals had skated by for 40 years, and were accustomed to living in denial.

Meanwhile, local officials kept 10,000 body bags in storage, while some estimated that a major storm could kill 100,000 people.

But it has to be admitted that there is nothing new about ignoring the results of wargames. The most famous example of this involves the Japanese navy in World War II. While planning a series of operations that resulted in the Battle of Midway in 1942, Japanese Admiral Yamamoto ran into a situation that showed his carriers were vulnerable to an American counterattack while launching attacks against the island. The incident was considered a fluke, and the lost carriers were resurrected in time to participate in operations later in the simulation. Of course, while readying an air strike against Midway on a June morning in 1942, while the carrier decks were crowded with fuel and bombs, U.S. Navy dive bombers swooped down and sank three of his carriers, later returning for the fourth and last. It would indeed have seemed like a fluke—had it not happened previously in the wargame, and if it did not turn out to be the decisive battle of the Pacific campaign.

Back on the Gulf Coast, the lessons of the Hurricane Pam wargame still apply. And at some level, nothing has changed since the exercise took place in 2004. A new hurricane season starts every June 1 in the Atlantic basin and lasts until November. Every year there is another roll of the dice, and another chance of a direct hit, and a new catastrophe.

Pam may still have prophecies up her sleeve.

20
Sirius and the Dogon

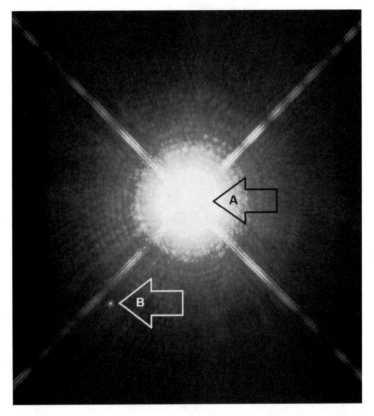

Sirius A, the brightest star in the night sky, and its tiny companion, Sirius B, in a Hubble space telescope image annotated by the author. NASA photo.

Sirius is the brightest star in the sky. On a given night, any points of light in the sky that are brighter than Sirius are certain to be planets, especially Venus or Jupiter—or satellites or airplanes, or (why not?) UFOs. Sirius is also called the Dog Star because it is the brightest star in the constellation Canis Major which is "Big Dog" in Latin. It starts appearing in the morning sky in late spring and is visible in the sky a little longer each night through the summer. The ancients assumed it contributed to the heat of the "dog days" of summer.

We now know that Sirius (about 8.6 light years away) is actually two stars, conveniently named Sirius A and B. Sirius A is the main star and Sirius B ("The Pup") is its tiny companion. Sirius B was discovered by accident in 1862 during testing of a new telescope of record-breaking size for the University of Chicago. It orbits Sirius B with a period of about 50 years, and its apparent separation from Sirius A, as seen from Earth, varies from 3 to 11.6 arcseconds.

And now we need to explain about the measurement of apparent separation, and put those measurements in perspective:

- The circle that surrounds you is divided into 360 degrees.
- An arcminute is 1-60th of a degree.
- An arcsecond is 1-60th of an arcminute.

As for perspective, one degree is about the apparent width (not length) of your little finger at arm's length. The apparent width of the full moon is half a degree, or 30 arcminutes. (Yes, despite its apparently impressive size as it looms over the trees, you can cover the moon with the tip of your outstretched little finger—try it.) A person with 20/20 vision should be able to distinguish a separation of one arcminute, or maybe a little less. The apparent width of the planet Jupiter varies but is usually about half an arcminute, or 30 arcseconds. It was not seen as a disc until the invention of the first astronomical telescope. Obviously, the apparent separation of Sirius A and B would fit inside the apparent diameter of Jupiter several times.

Meanwhile, the separation between Sirius A and Sirius B is enough to be discerned by a respectable backyard telescope (such as a six-inch reflector) but B is usually lost in the glare of A, which is approximately a thousand times brighter. Therefore special techniques are needed to see B. These techniques are usually based on foreknowledge of the existence and position of Sirius B.

The upshot of this exposition is that any pre-modern culture that pays any attention to seasonal changes in the sky would know about Sirius A. After all, it is the brightest star in the sky. But without telescopes there is no way they would know about Sirius B. No combination of clear air and visual acuity would permit them to see it.

So it was a little startling when claims surfaced that a pre-literate African tribe with no tradition of optical technology was found to know about Sirius B.

The tribe was the Dogon, residing in the Mopti region of Mali. Mali is a large land-locked country in West Africa, south of Algeria and north of the Ivory Coast. The Mopti region is in the middle of the country, and best known for the presence of the Niger River, for having the largest mosque in the world made out of mud, and for being on the road to Timbuktu. It was part of various shifting Saharan empires until the region fell under French control in the 1890s as part of French West Africa. It gained independence in 1960, but French is still the official language.

The story about the Dogon and their relationship with Sirius arose from writings of French anthologist Marcel Griaule, based on his interviews with a blind Dogon sage named Ogotemmeli in the late 1940s. The sage presented a sophisticated world view in which the surface manifestations of Dogon culture, and the physical world that surrounded them, merely reflected various aspects of a lengthy, complicated creation myth in which twinship and duality played central roles. Included was information about Sirius being a double star, including the orbital period of Sirius B. There was also mention of a third member of the system, which remains undiscovered.

Griaule was obviously fascinated, and the resulting ethnographic studies made him famous. He did not question the information, although some of the creation myths sound like rehashed Sunday school classes. For instance, heroes rebel against the creator, experience atonement, are saved from a flood by an ark, and suffer crucifixion. The story of Noah's drunkenness in the 9th chapter of Genesis also surfaces.

Generations of scholars and authors happily parroted his findings, rushing to use the Dogon to advance their world views. A sampling:

- The ancient Egyptians possessed telescopes and passed their findings on to the Dogon.
- Benevolent extraterrestrials must exist as they obviously passed the information on to the Dogon while passing through.
- Dark skin offers many advantages, such as letting you see better a night, especially in the desert.

While such assertions may have proven to be good things for the academic or publishing careers of certain individuals, others have expressed doubts. If the ancient Egyptians had telescopes, why was their heritage of astronomical knowledge passed on only to one tribe on the other side of Africa? If benevolent extraterrestrials were tutoring the Dogon, why didn't the little green men transmit some information that would be useful to the Dogon, such as how to build irrigation dams? (Speaking of that, Griaule was actually involved in local dam construction.) And since when does having dark skin give you eyeballs that are six inches wide? (That's what you need, by the way, to detect Sirius B.)

So it was no surprise in certain quarters when attempts in the 1990s to du-plicated Griaule's findings came up short. The researchers found members of the tribe with whom Griaule had worked, who recalled the way he never took "I don't know" for an answer. They would produce specific Dogon names for two dozen different types of dung beetles at a sitting, if that's what he wanted. Anyway, he was paying them.

The modern Dogons were mystified by Ogotemmeli's complex, subtle creation myth. If it represented some secret Dogon mysticism, they'd never heard of it. As for Sirius being a double star, they likewise had never heard of any such thing. They did assume that some stars were descended from oth-er brighter nearby stars—they were of different generations, in other words. Meanwhile, it's easy to confuse the French words *generation* and *giration* (meaning orbit), and the translators that Griaule was using were not univer-sity graduates. (Griaule, however, was, and was familiar with astronomy.)

Meanwhile, the Dogon had hardly been cut off from the outside world, as members of the tribe had been serving in the French army since World War I. Any one of them could have read an astronomy book, opening the floodgates of cross-cultural contamination.

In other words, what appears to be knowledge that is amazingly out of place is more likely knowledge that was firmly rooted in the present, coupled with pure noise. The noise has been generated by the interaction of two dif-ferent cultures, one of which was in the business of passing judgment on the other. Some of the people who listened to the noise have heard exactly what they wanted to hear, unrestrained by such repressive rhetorical concepts as truth, common sense, or a belief that one piece of information can be assigned greater value than another. There's no reverse anachronism or any challenge to the concept of linear time or technological progress.

But one point remains neglected: On a clear, still, moonless night in the desert, far away from urban sources of light pollution, the stars really are stunningly beautiful.

The Dogon surely knew that. How much more astronomy did they need?

LIVES AND CAREERS

Making predictions—even successful ones—is one thing. But what about living them? There have been people who have not only made correct predictions, but then lived their lives so as to make them happen.

Meanwhile, you'd think that successful prophecy would be an unbeatable career choice. After all, you can know in advance what works and what doesn't, and that should give you a major advantage over everyone else, who are wasting time and resources learning from hard experience. But judging from the examples gathered here, things like that don't really matter.

Among our examples, the most successful prophets in terms of career outcomes were considered either gadflies or curiosities, and no one beat a path to their door. The least successful were at best ignored, with their successors turning against them, pretending they never existed, or both. Additionally, one was mocked for not heeding his own prophecy, and another died wishing he'd been wrong.

But it's clear that they did not do what they did for the sake of making bystanders (or even themselves) feel better. Basically, they seemed to be consciously doing what they felt needed to be done in order for the envisioned future to come about.

This is either a very mysterious motivation, evident in only a few individuals in history, or it's the same reason you got up this morning. (You knew, didn't you, that another day would dawn? And that the new day would include specific events for which you had a envisioned a particular outcome?) With our examples, this motivation is simply played out on a vaster sale.

But don't believe me. Read on.

21
Inventing the Present

Douglas C. Engelbart, who spent years working to invent what we now know as the modern office, based on a vision he had while driving to work in 1951. Photo courtesy of SRI International.

Suppose you are driving to work, for an office job in California, and you have a vision—of yourself at a sort of computer-controlled visual display, one that employs symbology that represents your thinking, and that lets you navigate a landscape not of physical objects, but of information, while you are linked to collaborators anywhere on Earth.

You would probably just drive on to work, because the vision is just a summary of the way you spend your day at the office, with your desktop computer, its graphical interface, and its Internet connection.

But what if you had that vision in 1951?

Probably you'd just be confused. At the time computers were room-sized monsters used for special projects and were controlled through modified teletype machines. Live interaction with one, for any reason, was unheard of, even in the unlikely event you could find one west of the Mississippi River. Radar screens were the main example of electronic visual displays.

But if you were engineer Douglas C. Engelbart you would set out to make it real—and you would succeed, creating along the way a sizeable chunk of the modern world.

Born in 1925, Engelbart had served as a radar technician in the U.S. Navy at the end of World War II. While overseas he had come across Vannevar Bush's article "As We May Think" in a Red Cross library, with its emphasis on the need to employ technology to augment human intelligence.

In 1951 he was 25, he had his engineering degree and a steady job, and had gotten engaged. All his ambitions had been achieved—and he was unsettled about how superficial they turned out to be. He decided that he would find some way to better mankind while in the process supporting a family.

Then he had the vision.

The vision, and his related personal crusade, stayed with him through graduate school and finally in 1957 to a job at Stanford Research Institute (later SRI International). It took him a while to attain sufficient standing to get his own research funded, but eventually he did, leading to a paper titled "Augmenting Human Intelligence, A Conceptual Framework," prepared for the U.S. Air Force in 1962. It called for an environment in which human hunches, gut feelings, and other intangibles usefully coexisted with powerful analytic methods and electronic tools (that is, computers). This brought him a series of research grants from the Department of Defense Advanced Research Projects Agency (DARPA) and NASA.

NASA wanted advice on screen-selection devices, for use when controlling a computer in real time through a cathode ray tube (what we would call a computer monitor). Light pens were already available, but they involved repeatedly lifting the pen up and touching it to the screen, and that got tiresome. Engelbart's team experimented with a knee-operated pointer positioned under the desk, but that also got tiresome and lacked fine control. Various types of joysticks also proved unsatisfactory for various reasons.

Then they tried a small box with two sensor wheels that you pushed around the desk, rigged so that the screen cursor moved in a way that tracked the movements of the little box. The connector cord extend out the end and looked like a tail. It scored the best marks for usability, and people started calling it the mouse. The wheel later evolved into a rubber-coated steel ball, and then an optical sensor. Today you can also get wireless versions, seriously eroding the rationale for the name. The eventual patent was in the name of SRI and Engelbart did not get a penny.

Other developments came together at the so-called Mother of All Demos at a computer industry convention in San Francisco in late 1968, with about a thousand people watching in an auditorium thanks to an early projection monitor.

Engelbart demonstrated a system with screen editing, hypertext, a mouse with three buttons, a keyboard with special keys, long-distance links, integrated messages, and videoconferencing.

Screen editing, of course, is the basis of word processing, and what you type at in the cursor position pushes other text ahead of it. Previous text editors, typically based on paper output, were much cruder.

Hypertext (also called hyperlinks) are what the Internet uses to stitch together the World Wide Web. There being no Internet in its present form in 1968, Engelbart was using it to display elaborate footnotes, and to expand outlines.

The demo assumed that no one in the audience had seen a computer mouse before. His mouse had the previously described sensor wheels, and he noted that you could easily reposition around the desktop for comfort, and it stayed where you placed it. (He apologized for the name.) He actually had a mouse pad built into an indentation on the right side of his keyboard. He noted that his mouse was not accurate enough to trace something from paper to the screen, but most users simply watched the screen and adjusted their mouse movements to what they saw there.

The keyboard had several extra keys for computer control but otherwise had a standard four-row layout. But to the left, in a sort of additional indented mouse pad, there was a special five-button keypad that let you enter any letter through button combinations. (They were only using uppercase letters, so there were enough combinations with five buttons.)

The messaging system was closer to today's instant messaging than e-mail, but probably came as close to e-mail as they wanted or needed—at the time their system only had six terminals.

The teleconferencing was done with standard TV equipment that, under operator control, combined pictures of users and the contents of their screens. In other words, the video (and sound) was not processed digitally with the text and linked graphics, as would be done today.

Meanwhile, his text editor had facilities that let two people work on text at the same time, for collaboration purposes.

As for the Internet, Engelbart mentioned that his lab was working with the experimental ARPANET, with the intention of making the facilities he was demonstrating available through remote links.

He got a standing ovation. More than that, an industry arose around his ideas. About the only thing that he demonstrated that day that you don't find in modern offices is that five-key keyboard, and possibly live collaboration. As for that five-finger device, everyone these days is assumed to be able to use a QWERTY keyboard, and the use of both upper and lowercase letters makes five keys inadequate. Live collaboration, meanwhile, usually involves more micromanagement than is comfortable.

The ARPANET has matured into the Internet and its World Wide Web. (Engelbart's lab was one of the original four nodes on the ARPANET/Internet.) With its associated e-mail facilities, the Internet has become indispensible in many business and industrial settings—you cannot do business without access. But thanks to various market forces, powerful personal computers can be acquired for the cost of a moderately fancy television set.

The advent of the personal computer meant that those who continued to believe in multi-user environments found themselves with smaller and smaller audiences. This included Engelbart, who branched into management seminars, consulting, and occasional development contracts as his research funding dried up in the 1980s. At this writing he has his own nonprofit organization, the Doug Engelbart Institute, to further research on ways to augment human intelligence.

If his visions constituted a reverse anachronism, then Engelbart must be one of the few people to have made a career out of one. But it might be fairer to say that anyone moved by Vannevar Bush's article, knew what computers could do, and who was used to working with radar displays, might have had similar musings. Engelbart, however, felt that the vision was worth pursuing—and did manage to bring it to life. Today, office workers do sit in front of visual computer terminals, manipulate symbology-based controls (they're called icons) and navigate an informational landscape (it's called the Internet).

Has his creation succeeded? Can we actually augment human intelligence? Or have we simply made paperwork mercilessly fast while bemusing ourselves with Google search results? It's probably fair to say that we have been able to explore the potential of this new environment about as thoroughly as Gutenberg was personally able to explore the potential offered by moveable type.

In other words, check back in a few centuries.

Meanwhile, if you have any odd, technology-based visions while driving to work, you might consider heeding them.

22
Personal Reverse Anachronism

Chief Plenty Coups of the Crow, who led his people based on a boyhood vision that told him that the white men would sweep away the Indian tribes and that their cattle would replace the buffalo. Public domain image from Wikimedia Commons.

What do you do when you are sure that you have been given information about the future—which is that your way of life is going to be destroyed? Doubt your sanity and shut up? Run around like Chicken Little announcing that the sky is falling until bystanders suppress you? Or accept your vision as genuine foreknowledge, and see that your culture benefits from it?

Among the Plains Indians of the 19th century there was actually a mechanism for bringing about the latter outcome. One man leveraged it for the benefit of his tribe, while all around him others succumbed to the white conquest.

He was a member of the Crow Nation born about 1848 named Aleek-chea-ahoosh, meaning Plenty Coups. A coup (pronounced "coo") was a recognized act of flaunted bravery, such as disarming an enemy in battle, or stealing a horse from an enemy camp. The practice of "counting coup" did not mean that they saw war as a sport. Rather, it allowed them to derive some personal meaning from the murderous, eternal tribal wars that shaped their existence. Meanwhile, a man had to have counted coup at least once before he was allowed to get married before the age of 25. After age 25 a man who had never counted coup was free to marry—but his wife was not allowed to paint her face.

The cultural mechanism for change derived from their belief in visions. Every warrior was supposed to have one, usually brought on by solitary fasting and exposure. What the warrior saw during his vision set the tone for his life and usually indicated what animal spirits he was to call on when in distress.

Plenty Coups had his defining vision at age 11. At the direction of a mysterious figure in a buffalo robe with the hair on the outside, he saw countless buffalo pour out of a hole in the ground, spread out across the plains—and then disappear. Then a different herd of strange animals emerged from the hole and covered the plain, with different markings, longer tails, and making different sounds.

Then he was shown an old man sitting in the shade by a house—the same house he would later occupy in old age.

Then he saw a dark forest assailed by powerful winds that tore down all the trees except one. A tiny chickadee lived in that tree. The mysterious figure assured Plenty Coups that the chickadee was a good listener, who learned how others succeeded or failed, without trouble to himself.

After Plenty Coups awoke, recuperated, and returned to the village, a tribal council convened to hear his vision, as was typically done. He was urged to tell everything he had seen, and assured that, if he was too young to understand, there were others present who could.

When he was through describing his vision, the officiating chief lit a pipe and passed it around the room, from east to west like the sun. It went around the room four times without a word being spoken.

Finally, the leader announced an interpretation: Within the lifetime of Plenty Coups, the buffalo would be gone, replaced by the cattle of the white men. Those tribes who opposed white expansion would be destroyed, like the forest in the vision. But the Crow, who were often outnumbered by their enemies, could survive if they listened and learned like the chickadee. The Crow were then the only tribe that had not warred with the whites, and they must strive to remain friends with them.

And that was how it worked out in the coming decades. Things came to a head in the summer of his 29th year when Plenty Coups was already a chief. The bluecoat Limping Soldier came to ask for help in a war against the ancestral enemies of the Crow: the Sioux, the Cheyenne, and the Arapahoe. The Crow chiefs agreed, as they were eager to demonstrate their friendship with the whites, in keeping with Plenty Coups' vision. Crow warriors were sent to act as scouts for Son-of-the-Morning-Star and The-Other-One. Plenty Coups himself went with a sizable Crow force to the camp of Three-Stars.

The terrain was crawling with enemy scouts, like lice on a buffalo robe, and Plenty Coups thought Three-Stars did not understand the severity of the situation. First Three-Stars was waiting for messengers who were unlikely to get through, and then he marched straight toward the massed Sioux on Rosebud Creek when he could have gone around. The resulting big fight did not go well and they had to retreat back to Three-Star's wagon camp.

Things were worse with Son-of-the-Morning-Star, who did not wait for Three-Stars or The-Other-One but divided his men into groups and attacked an enemy village that was far too big for him. When the Crow scout Half-Yellow-Face saw what Son-of-the-Morning-Star was doing he began stripping and applying funeral face paint. Son-of-the-Morning-Star asked why he was doing that.

"Because you and I are going home today, and by a trail that is strange to both of us," Half-Yellow-Face replied. Annoyed, Son-of-the-Morning-Star sent Half-Yellow-Face away, and so Half-Yellow-Face survived that day.

Incidentally, Plenty Coup's 29th year was 1876. The Limping Soldier was Col. John Gibbon (wounded twice in the U.S. Civil War), while Three-Stars was Gen. George Crook. The big fight that Plenty Coups fought in, which did not go well, was the Battle of the Rosebud, and was the largest battle of the Indian Wars on the plains. Son-of-the-Morning-Star was Gen. George Custer, who was indeed supposed to wait for The-Other-One (Gen. Alfred Terry) and Three-Stars. The enemy village he found was on the Little Bighorn River, and the fight that Half-Yellow-Face was excused from is known as Custer's Last Stand.

Although the soldiers were unlucky they did cripple the enemies of the Crow, and Plenty Coups' people were thereafter able to sleep soundly at night, without fear of attack. Later, the Crows were granted an Indian reservation on land they already considered their own, while the tribes that had been hostile to the whites got land they despised.

As well as a tribal leader, Plenty Coups later had careers as a tribal lobbyist and businessman, always stressing that, for the modern Crow warrior, education was the preferred weapon. He dictated his memoirs in about 1928. The end came in 1932.

As for an explanation, perhaps the tribal leaders were already leaning toward a pro-white policy when young Plenty Coups described his vision, and seized on the spectral backing it offered, perhaps even convincing the boy that he had seen what they wanted him to see. But that does not explain his lifelong commitment to a policy that assumed the destruction of the way of life he knew at the time when he experienced the vision.

Or maybe we should consider a comment in his memoirs: There are things that we do not understand. When we encounter them it is best to acknowledge them and leave them alone.

The author's mother was introduced to Chief Plenty Coup as a young girl much as, in other cultures, children are presented to royalty. She remembers they were pronouncing the P in *coups*, as she was wondering how many chickens (who live in coops) he had. And that the sight of children, including the daughter of a white gas station manager like herself, made him smile.

23
Akhenaten

Heretic monotheistic pharaoh Akhenaten depicted under the rays of the Aten with one of his wives and three of his children. Wikimedia Commons image by Keith Schengili-Roberts. Used under license.

Monotheism—the acceptance of one supreme creator-being and the rejection of all other forces of supernatural power—was supposedly invented by Abraham about 1100 BC. Judaism, Christianity, and Islam can be traced directly to this invention, although there are unrelated monotheistic religions, such as Sikhism.

And then there's Akhenaten, an Egyptian pharaoh who set up his own monotheistic religion around 1350 BC. His religion did not survive him—in fact, later pharaohs literally tried to erase his memory. They were so successful that nothing was known about him until archeologists began excavating the ruins of an isolated, abandoned city on the east side of the Nile about 150 years ago.

They found that the city, called Amarna, had been built by Amenhotep IV, starting about 1347 BC. At the same time he began practicing a religion that venerated a lone deity named Aten, and changed his name to Akhenaten, or Pleasing-to-Aten. Aten, represented by the orb of the sun and its life-giving rays, was soon declared the sole creator-being. The rites of the old gods, whose priests and scribes had run Egypt for 15 centuries, were abandoned. The rites of the new god was celebrated in the open, whereas the old gods had been worshiped in dark seclusion.

His abandonment of the old ways also included a more relaxed style of portraiture, although it was apparently no more lifelike than the old stiff, formulaic style. He and his family are shown in ordinary settings, but are depicted with an odd combination of masculine and feminine features, plus pot bellies and elongated faces and heads. Because these features are absent on his presumed mummy, it is assumed that the artists were assigning features that, under the new religion, implied special status. (Anyway, for security purposes, the pharaohs may have been uninterested in the public knowing what they really looked like.)

Nor did he abandon all the old ways—he remained married to his sister, for instance, and took at least one other wife as well.

Part of Akhenaten's diplomatic correspondence survived in one Amarna building. These indicate that religion was not a foreign policy issue. Instead, the recurring theme (oddly familiar today) was a chorus of demands for military assistance by allied states in the Middle East, whose ruling warlords were alarmed by their aggressive neighbors and restive peasants. (There were also reports of plagues. Tracking them may have been an ongoing task for any pharaoh's intelligence service.)

Akhenaten died in the 17th year of his reign—and the Aten religion was almost immediately abandoned. After some turmoil kingship fell to the boy Tutankhaten (Living-Image-of-Aten), who (or the regents who controlled him) soon restored the status of the old religion. In fact, Tutankhaten changed his name to Tutankhamun (Living-Image-of-Amun, Amun being the chief god of the old religion). He then married his half sister, abandoned Amarna, and moved his court back to the old capital of Thebes. As anyone who has perused a King-Tut museum display can attest, he was in due course buried with all the trappings of the old religion.

Sometime after that they chiseled Akhenaten's name off the monuments (outside derelict Amarna, anyway), removed his name from the dynastic list, and commenced pretending that he had never existed. For more than 30 centuries it worked.

Or maybe it didn't. Today, monotheistic religions are the norm. They have no obvious link to Akhenaten, but consider this: In one tomb in Amarna researchers found a poem now called "The Great Hymn of the Aten." It lauds the beauty and orderliness of creation, which it describes as the work of a single creator and supreme being, Aten. Scholars often compare it to Psalm 104, which has the same theme and general structure, minus references to Aten. King David presumably wrote that and other psalms about 350 years after Akhenaten, so some influence is possible.

Akhenaten also continues to influence us through the painted limestone bust of his non-sister wife, Nefertiti, whose lifelike, regal pose make it one of the most arresting artifacts ever found in Egypt. (We have no idea if it really looked like her, of course.) It was unearthed in a ruined Amarna workshop in 1912 by German archeologists whose Indiana Jones–style methods of getting it out of the country continue to generate Egyptian demands for its return.

And he also lives on in a cottage industry that has tried to explain his actions. It's clear that he tried to accomplish a genuine revolution. The usual motive for such a move is that the old regime is corrupt and unresponsive—but that does not explain the features of the religion he founded, seemingly out of thin air. The simplest explanation is that he was sincere in his beliefs—and that the old regime was corrupt and unresponsive.

Did he have access to some kind of foreknowledge? Probably not. A time traveler with religious motivations would surely proselyte his or her own religion to Akhenaten. Because Aten-ism is not currently practiced that rules out Akhenaten's career as a reverse anachronism of the first kind (that is, from the present). But that does not rule out the possibility of it being a reverse anachronism of the second kind (that is, from the future) because we can't know what beliefs will hold sway in the distant future. Meanwhile, it's intriguing that Akhenaten's artists represented Aten as an orb, because they could not have known that the sun was a sphere rather than a disc. Of course, their decision to use a sphere could have been accidental, and no more representational than the appearance of Akhenaten and his family.

Our time traveler would probably also have urged Akhenaten to watch his back with the old guard, and not pressure the man on the street into changing religions. But Akhenaten probably did not need the former advice, and archeological evidence of numerous personal old-religion amulets in Amarna indicated he followed the latter advice.

Advising him to give up incest, wise as it would have been, may not have been realistic, considering his emotional investment in the system. Hawaiian royalty, for instance, was slow to give it up, for similar reasons.

And our traveler would certainly have urged him to set an enduring precedent, and tell those Middle East warlords to learn to live with each other. But Akhenaten would have known that some things are just too much to ask.

24
More Lifeboats

British journalist W.T. Stead, who wrote about the dangers of passenger ships not carrying enough lifeboats. He then booked passage on the RMS Titanic. *Public domain image from Wikimedia Commons.*

There were lifeboats for only about 1/3 of the people on board the passenger liner—or so they realized after a collision in the middle of the Atlantic. The crew had drilled with lifeboats while the passengers just watched. When it came time to abandon ship they botched the launching of the lifeboats, in some cases managing to get few if anyone on board, while they also literally fought to enforce the "women and children first" drill. When they ran out of boats there were still about 700 people on the ship, who had to try to swim for it through the deadly cold water as the ship made its death plunge.

If you want a summation of the sinking of the *Titanic* in 1912, the previous paragraph might suffice—except for two details. The first is that the number of the doomed people stuck on board the *Titanic* totaled about 1,500 rather than 700. The second detail is that the paragraph is not a summary of the *Titanic*'s sinking, but of the plot of a short story titled "'How the Mail Steamer Went Down in mid-Atlantic' By a Survivor," in the March 22, 1886, edition of the *Pall Mall Gazette* by journalist and social activist W.T. Stead.

In other words, Stead's description of the disaster came out 26 years before it took place. That said, it's time to point out that his clairvoyance was not crystal clear. In his story, chaos broke out after the collision, whereas class-bound behavior codes kept a damper on panic during the real disaster. But the big difference was that his fictional ship collided with another ship, whereas the real disaster involved a collision with an iceberg.

As if to make up for this, in 1892 he went on to write a travelogue novel titled *From the Old World to the New*, whose plot devices included a person rescued from a ship that sank after hitting an iceberg.

By 1912 he owned multiple magazines, but his heart was still in social crusades. When he decided to attend an anti-war conference in the United States, of course he got a first-class ticket on a passenger liner. There was no reason not to choose the newest, largest, and most comfortable one available.

Well, actually there was a reason—one that should have been familiar to Stead.

What could he have been thinking? Had he really put the issue out of his mind? Did he not pause to count the lifeboats as he boarded the vessel, the RMS *Titanic*? They were hung from davits that were actually designed to handle stacks of four boats, but someone didn't get the memo, and there was only one lifeboat per set of davits. Altogether there were 20 lifeboats of all kinds, with a capacity of 1,178 people, or about a third of the ship's rated capacity. The fictional ship in his short story had had 916 people on board, and space in eight lifeboats for 390 people.

After stopping in France and Ireland, the *Titanic* had 2,240 on board when she headed into the Atlantic. Stead sent a postcard to a business associate when the ship stopped in France. And that's the last thing that we know for sure about him. Various accounts have him retiring to his room to write and drink tea after the collision, while the crew botched the loading of the few lifeboats, just as in his story.

How did Stead spend his last moments? Did he ponder the irony of the situation? If he had been in a mood to pause and reflect on his life and work, a short story ranting about marine safety decades earlier may not have even come to mind. Indeed, for him it may have been one of the more forgettable things he had done—and would be for us were it not for the fatal irony. But what little evidence we have indicates that he was fully "in the moment" and not dwelling on the past.

That's because some accounts have him stepping out onto the sloping deck toward the end, requesting that the band (one of whose members was the son of an acquaintance) perform a hymn he had heard played at state funerals, "Nearer, My God, to Thee." President McKinley had supposedly muttered its words while dying in 1901. To moderns, it seems odd that playing a funeral hymn during a moment of extreme and obvious mortal peril was considered a good idea. But the Victorians upheld the ideal of the "good death," according to which the actions of a person in peril took on spiritual significance after he or she signaled the full acceptance of death. Maybe the playing of the hymn was his signal.

But if he did dwell on the past, there was plenty to think about. Basically, William Thomas Stead (born in 1849) had been a founding figure in investigative journalism, and along the way pioneered the genre of interview stories. In 1883 he became editor of the *Pall Mall Gazette*, an evening newspaper in London. In pre-Internet times morning newspapers concentrated on news, while evening newspapers snagged their readers with human interest features, entertainment, and muck-raking—and that sometimes meant creating news rather than just reporting it. Stead, it turns out, was not above that. Meanwhile, Stead did not approve of the conspiracy of silence that Victorians enforced about all things involving sex, because he knew that it gave abusers a cloak of invisibility.

The two trends came together in 1885 when Stead got fed up with Parliament for proving unable to pass a bill that would raise the age of consent from 13 all the way to 16 and impose other measures meant to suppress child prostitution. The result was a lurid series in his newspaper, filled with first-person accounts from informants recruited through the Salvation Army, titled, "The Maiden Tribute of Modern Babylon." It ripped the lid off the child prostitution underworld and named lawmakers who stopped the bill, implying hidden agendas. The phrase "maiden tribute" was used in the sense of "girls sent as sacrifices to a foreign power" rather than the modern usage of "marks of respect bestowed on unmarried women." The girls ultimately ended up in "pleasure palaces" in Europe, the series reported.

Many newsstands would not carry the editions, and crowds besieged outlets where they were available.

Parliament soon caved in, but Stead found he had made powerful enemies. The series included an account of the purchase from her mother of a 13-year-old girl for five pounds, who was then lightly drugged, taken to a brothel, and presented to a paying client. The "client" turned out to be Stead himself, who had set up the transaction through intermediaries as part of his research for the article. He left the room, without contact, after the girl woke up screaming. (Incidentally, the padded walls of such establishments were designed to muffle the girls' screams, readers learned.) The authorities could show that she had been removed from her home without the permission of her putative father, and jailed Stead for three months for abduction. He found incarceration to be restful, and it did not interfere with his editorial work. He kept his prison uniform as a souvenir, although he apparently had not bothered to wear it while in prison.

His credentials thus established, he went on to establish a muck-raking monthly magazine called *Review of Reviews* in 1890, and this gradually turned into a small publishing empire, including a very successful American version of the magazine that lasted until 1936. He also got into spiritualism, anti-war activism, and the promotion of Esperanto, a constructed language (still in circulation) intended for international use. He made waves by not only hiring women for professional positions, but also for paying them the same as men. He was even known to address them as equals.

During his lifetime most wars involving Europeans were imperial adventures rather than catastrophic big-power collisions, so his anti-war stance sometimes ran counter to public opinion in imperial England. During the Boer War he was openly pro-Boer, and his magazine suffered severely. The situation appears to have stabilized by 1912, and he was hoping to meet President Taft when he boarded the *Titanic* for an anti-war conference in Chicago.

So, as the water rose and the band played on, whatever he was thinking about probably did not involve a filler piece he whipped out after he got out of jail and before he founded his magazine. And most certainly he was not pondering the ultimate irony: that 100 years later he would be better known for going down with the *Titanic* in a manner he had himself indirectly predicted, than for anything he had fought for or accomplished before then.

When the rescue ship got to New York it was met with messages for Stead from editors franticly wanting his first-person account of the disaster, offering top rates. They got no response, of course. But you have to wonder if he would have bothered to respond even if he had survived.

After all, he'd already written that story, and had moved on.

25
A Cartoonist Gets It Right

Albert Robida, the French cartoonist
who predicted, among other things,
videoconferencing, air travel, and
women's liberation. Public domain
file from Wikimedia Commons.

Of course you've heard of 19th-century French science fiction writer Jules Verne. (No? See Chapter 6.) His characters pondered every detail and specification of whatever marvelous invention was in play until the reader could not avoid feeling educated. The plots seemed secondary. Some things he got stunningly correct. But one thing he never did was illustrate his work.

For that we have his almost forgotten contemporary, the shy, nearsighted, and astonishingly prolific Albert Robida (1848–1926). Robida's illustrated stories are swarming with marvelous inventions that are given just enough scientific explanation to assure the reader that they are not magic and can be expected to behave in a consistent manner. Of course, this is the relationship that most people in the real world have with most of the real technology around them. His plots could often get by without the inventions, because they were based on social issues. He was obviously trying to entertain (often with underplayed social satire) rather than teach introductory engineering. But as for his predictions—well, often the modern reader only needs to make minor adjustments and change certain names to make Robida's world fit the present.

His premiere work of futurism is probably *The Twentieth Century* (*Le Vingtième Siècle*), a handsomely bound, heavily illustrated book that was released for the 1882 Christmas season. Supposedly, it included material and ideas he had been amassing for the previous 11 years while supporting himself and a growing family doing magazine, caricature, and commercial illustration. In other words, it was material he had been distracting himself with since his miraculous survival of the bloody suppression of the leftist Paris Commune insurrection that flared for two months at the end of the Franco-Prussian War of 1870–71. Not a man of any overt political convictions, he had simply been trapped in Paris when it was surrounded by the Prussian army. After revolution swept the city he had been appointed to an administrative post in the rebel government as a result of personal connections. Eventually the Prussian army stepped aside and the French army retook the city, one barricaded street at a time. Thousands who had served the Commune suffered summary execution. The story is that Robida just walked away from the firing squad, and his absent-minded demeanor let him fit in as a bystander.

In other words, having seen a world destroyed, he set about creating a new one in considerable detail.

The resulting opus concerns the dilemma faced by recent high school graduate Helene Colobry in the autumn of 1952. An orphan, she is the ward of a distant rich uncle who tells her that she must now settle on a career and get a job. It's a scene that has been lived out with many young men—but she's a young woman. When she starts to say she had not made any career plans, feels no call to any career, and had expected—he won't let her finish, noting that all careers are now open to women, while implying that she needs to pull her weight and not depend on finding a husband to support her.

So she goes out into the world and tries one career after another. Yes, they are all open to women now—and the joke is that the presence of women ultimately changes nothing. Regardless of their gender, everyone pursues their job in a happy-go-lucky yet earnest manner that is a wide-eyed cross between manic and naive. The implied irony is that all the fears about feminism are groundless. She tries law (too distasteful), politics (the training is simultaneously too boring and too demanding), journalism (too many duels and/or marriage proposals), and finance (too much math). But despite everything, she does eventually achieve her unstated goal of marital bliss, after rescuing her intended from a jail for holdout bachelors in polygamous Mormon Britain.

Meanwhile, she is surrounded by artifacts of advanced technology—which is not the same as saying she is surrounded by artifacts of advanced science, because she is not familiar with much of the science behind the artifacts. Basically, Robida dwells on functions, not explanations, but the functions tend to form a grand whole that underpins his imagined society. (He does sometimes note that a particular thing runs on electricity.)

To moderns, his most convincing artifact is probably telecommunications—his heroes are locked in a web of communications, and news from all over the world impacts their affairs. He envisions a dual network of nearly ubiquitous telephones, and less common telephonoscopes. His telephones function pretty much as the modern versions do, while the telephonoscope is a two-way voice and video transceiver that can be dialed to communicate two-way with any other telephonoscope. It can be used for shopping and telecommuting as well as personal communication. In other words, it's Internet videoconferencing in all but name. If there was data access as well there would be no question of calling it the Internet.

In receive-only mode the telephonoscope can display broadcasts of theatrical events, and is a flat-panel TV in all but name.

He mentions air travel with speeds equivalent to modern jet liners. But his illustrations show blimps that could never travel at such speeds (and are too small for their payloads). Railroads have been replaced by faster pneumatic tubes, extending even under the English Channel. Local travel is by less-convincing aero-cabs, which he sometimes refers to as helicopters but (in the illustrations) have no wings or rotors of any kind. Apparently they levitate like the transports in *Star Wars*.

North America has been divided between Chinese and German empires—except the Mormon Republic buffer state, which colonized England after the British government relocated to India. He skewers French politics by having the French nation spend three months every 10 years staging a choreographed, constitutionally mandated revolution that actually overthrows the government. The event is loud, with barricades being erected and stormed. But, thanks to careful planning, it's essentially bloodless, and most citizens see it as an excuse for a vacation. (Obviously, he's having the nation re-enact the Commune experience, and reduce it to an absurdity.)

The book is riddled with other predictions that Robida probably felt were equally silly—but we may not always agree:

- A ruinous series of wars broke out in 1910. *He was off by four years.*

- Russia was destroyed (sunk into the sea) by revolutionaries using weapons of mass destruction in 1920. *That would be more succinct than describing the impact of the revolution, Stalinist purges, and the Nazi invasion and genocide.*

- Punishment in the correctional system involves (in ascending seriousness) time-outs, sabbaticals, or retirement in special retirement homes where infractions are punished by withdrawing dessert. *Today's politicians are more likely to be "tough on crime."*

- Pianos are considered instruments of torture and no longer used. *Loud music has been used to enhance interrogations in the present day.*

- Manufactured food is piped into houses. *We have to drive to retail outlets to acquire it now.*

- Hemlines have gone up, as career women cannot submit to the oppression of long dresses. *They've shown variability. Experts differ as to why.*

- Recorded performances of dead entertainers of all sorts are played on special occasions. *Classic movies are widely available.*

- The telephonoscope can be dialed to saucy fare (plainly marked as such) that proper young ladies ought not to be allowed to watch. *Got cable?*

- The use of electricity greatly reduces the need for servants. *That's true.*

- Whole nations have declared bankruptcy. *That has happened.*

- Italy has been turned into a huge theme park. *Euro Disney is not that big.*

- Anyone who cannot make it in any other career is advised to go into politics. *The results speak for themselves.*

- A lot of courtship takes place by telephone. *You could call it courtship.*

- Tiny hearing aids could be worn almost invisibly. *We have that.*

- Telephone sets are everywhere, so you can reach anyone at any time. *Cell phones accomplish the same thing.*

- Advertising is everywhere, including product placements in theatrical performances. *We certainly have that.*

- Theatrical performances are given in multiple languages simultaneously. *Movies on DVDs often have multiple language options.*

- Most young ladies are pretty, dress fashionably, and have hour-glass figures. *Who is to say otherwise?*

Taken as a whole, Robida was too early. The telecommunications environment that he described was closer to 2002 than 1952, and his levitating cabs are not here yet. (Of course, more banal wheeled ground transportation achieves the same result today, at about the same pace.) Meanwhile, if he did have some genuine foreknowledge of the future, he would have mentioned radio and antibiotics, because his characters get into situations in which those inventions would have been useful.

And he would also have foreseen the horrific nature of what was to happen in 1914, which transcended any of his predictions. He lived to see it, and of his seven children, one was killed and two were maimed at the front. In 1925 he gave an interview saying how he hated the hectic pace of modern life—a pace he had predicted. He died a year later after a short illness.

Very likely he preferred the 19th century over the 20th—even if, in a sense, he invented it.

26
Pre-Computer Programmer

*Ada Byron King, the Countess of Lovelace,
who managed to become the world's first programmer even though she lived a century before the
first programmable computers became available.
Public domain image from Wikimedia Commons.*

Her name was Ada Augusta King (nee Byron) the Right Honorable the Countess of Lovelace. She was young. She was beautiful. She was brilliant, especially at mathematics—they called her "the enchantress of numbers." She wrote the world's first known published computer program, in 1843.

That's right, in 1843.

In other words, she wrote a computer program about a century before the first programmable computer was available. But it wasn't her fault—she was actually planning for one to be invented.

Let's explain: From childhood Ada (1815–1852) was trained in advanced math by her mother. This was unusual at the time for a young English lady of aristocratic blood, but math had been an avocation for her aristocratic mother—and her mother additionally wanted to instill interests in the girl that were polar opposites of those displayed by her father. That's because Ada's father was the famous poet Lord Byron, a towering figure of the literary school of Romanticism. Memorable works that you might have read in school include "She Walks in Beauty" and "Childe Harold's Pilgrimage." Not included in the literature textbooks are the handful of speeches he made in the House of Lords—more on that later.

Byron's tumultuous, frenzied, and rather unfocused love life continues to challenge the skills of biographers, especially in the employment of euphemisms. Mrs. Byron felt especially challenged, and threw him out when Ada was only a month old. He soon took his adventuring overseas, never to return. He died when Ada was 9 years old.

Despite or because of her genetics, it turned out that Ada loved math, and displayed a genuine aptitude for it. In her teens she was sent to London to "attend court," meaning hang out in high society and find a husband. ("Court" meant the aristocratic and royal social circle, not the place where trials were held.) Math tutoring continued via correspondence. Meanwhile, to avoid having to answer questions, she was careful to avoid the presence of another young lady about her age and appearance who was also attending court. Ada's father had fathered the other girl with his married half-sister—one example of the pressing need for euphemisms when it comes to Lord Byron.

At age 17, in 1833, Ada was at a party where Charles Babbage spoke about his project, the Difference Engine. As noted in I-7, Babbage was trying to develop a mechanical means of producing math tables that were not riddled with errors. Such tables were important navigational tools, and reliable navigation was important to the British seafaring economy and to its navy. Consequently Babbage had been able to get some government backing, but by 1833 it was becoming obvious that the project was stalled.

There or soon afterwards Babbage showed her working components of the Difference Engine and started talking about his next project, which involved expanding the project into what he called the Analytical Engine. It would have the ability to store and execute instructions encoded on punched cards, using data that was itself encoded on punched cards. The results would be printed on paper by the machine itself. The instructions could include loops, branches, and conditional branches. We would call it a computer, although its workings were purely mechanical and therefore thousands of times slower than its electronic descendents more than a century later.

We would also call it a product of "creeping featurism," as its creators abandoned an unfinished project for an expanded version of the unfinished project, and the new project was itself never finished. Ada, of course, cannot be blamed for missing the warning signs of amateur management of an information technology development project, this being the first information technology development project ever attempted.

The point is that she was entranced with the project from the day she encountered it and remained associated with it thereafter. Meanwhile, the next year she married the future Earl of Lovelace and had three children by 1839. This did not help her health, which had already been tenuous.

In 1840 Babbage made his one and only foreign presentation about the Analytical Engine, to a group in Turin, Italy. A local professor of mathematics, Federico Menabrea (1809–1896), took notes and published an account of it, in French, in a Swiss journal. He went on to enter politics, and was prime minister of Italy from 1867 to 1869. He did not commit the Italian nation to any information technology development projects.

Babbage asked Ada (by then a countess, as the wife of an earl is styled) to translate the article. She did, but then added a series of seven notes, A through G, that, with 19,200 words, were more than twice as long as the original article (which had 8,100 words). Published in *Scientific Memoirs*, a journal that reprinted articles from foreign scientific societies and universities, it was the first scientific paper ever devoted to the topic of computer science.

There would not be another one for about a century.

Note G usually gets the most attention, as it lays out in considerable detail the procedures that the machine would use to calculate Bernoulli numbers. These were special fractions used to compute the sum of consecutive integer powers and were useful in making math tables. They also show up in number theory and topology. The process of producing them involves a lot of repetitive simple calculations, making the process a good example of what the Analytical Engine could do.

The resulting program was not a computer program in the sense that it was written in the coded notation of some formalized software language, like Fortran or C. No such languages would be formalized until the 1950s. Instead, Ada's "program" was a step-by-step description of what needed to be done to solve the problem, but it was detailed and unambiguous enough that it could be immediately rewritten in a computer language.

Basically, it was a huge loop that walked through each operation the machine would need to perform in order to produce a Bernoulli number, with the ability to loop back and start over with the next Bernoulli number, generating as many as desired using the same set of instructions. The description was detailed enough that later commentators were able to show that she left out a counting variable and mislabeled another variable—the first software bugs!

The article stressed that any calculation of any complexity could be performed. She also suggested that the machine would be used to compose (not generate) elaborate music by feeding it the rules of harmony and musical composition.

Ada also spent a few lines explaining that machines don't think. The Analytical Engine could perform analysis if told to do so, following programmed steps, but could not anticipate the issues involved in the analysis. Whole books were devoted to the topic of computer non-thought during the early days of the computer revolution, but the issue apparently seems self-evident to later generations who were raised with computers and computerized video games.

Babbage never got funding and his Analytical Engine was never built, beyond a few test components. Copies of a later version of his simpler Difference Engine were later built, long after his death, and worked as he said they would.

As for Ada, her health began to decline after publication of the paper, and she died in 1852 of what is now assumed to have been uterine cancer.

Her name lives on in a programming language called Ada which was commissioned by the Pentagon and began circulating in 1983. It was intended to do away with the Babel of programming languages the U.S. military was then using, and was designed to be highly structured. That means that, with Ada, you can't write sloppy spaghetti code that's too dense to debug, even if you tried. It was pretty much required for military projects until 1997, when they opened the door to cheap off-the-shelf commercial components without regard to the software language. Ada is still used, however—the military will always love structure.

In the end, Ada the software language has probably not put anybody out of work, and that would have pleased Lord Byron, the father of the real Ada. Those speeches he made in the House of Lords were mostly in favor of the followers of Nedd Ludd, who were rioting in English mill towns against the introduction of automated looms. These used instructions coded on punched cards to wave complex patterns into cloth, which put skilled weavers out of work.

When Ada's vision finally became a reality about a century after her death, the new analytical engines also used punched cards, and those who opposed automation were called luddites. Serious scientists cited Ada's work. Everything seemed to be coming around again—except for some new retro Byronic narrative poetry whose cantos of iambic pentameter cut through the post-modern verbal clutter.

We're still waiting for that.

27
Not in California

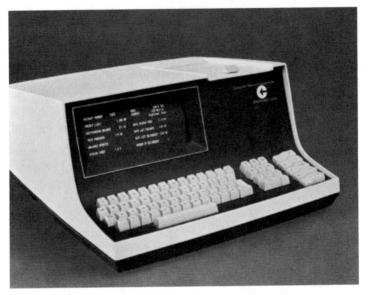

The Datapoint 2200, the 1970 desktop computer from which all x86 computers directly descend. Launched before the microprocessor revolution, and originating outside California, it has been disregarded by history. Public domain image courtesy of Austin Roche.

Over and over, from the late 1960s into the late 1990s, the questions would suddenly bubble to the surface, usually at random moments in telephone conversations that were supposedly about something else. When talking to outsiders, executives at Computer Terminal Corp., later renamed Datapoint Corp., would hear it again and again:

"Where in California is San Antonio located?" "Is there an airport nearby?" "Is there a large city nearby?"

It happened literally on the first call the company's cofounder made to a supplier shortly after it started operations in 1968, and never ended. The callers found it inconceivable that they were talking to a leading-edge computer company in sleepy, forgotten, semi-colonial San Antonio, Texas.

Meanwhile, at the same time, the legend of California's Silicon Valley was growing, about how Intel developed the first microprocessor chip, the 4004, in

1971, and about how Steve Jobs used a later microprocessor in the first mass-produced personal desktop computer, the Apple II, in 1977, opening the flood-gates of the computer revolution.

It's a comforting legend that leaves no loose ends, constructed in part by the participants. And it's wrong—sleepy San Antonio, Texas, is where it all began. (It does have a large airport, incidentally.) CTC/Datapoint triggered the microprocessor revolution and was able to ride that increasingly important technological innovation to a point where the firm promised to be a major participant in a new industrial—indeed, social—revolution. And then it crashed in flames, leaving the Californians to continue their myth-making unimpeded.

They were pioneers and mavericks, metaphorically akin to early San Antonio settler and entrepreneur Sam Maverick (1803–1870), from whom we get the dictionary entry. (Some of his descendents were apparently among the original investors, although a definitive list has not surfaced.) But pioneers sometimes get arrows in the chest.

It all started in 1967 (while Steve Jobs was still in middle school) when NASA engineers Phil Ray (1935–1987) and Gus Roche (1929–1975) decided that the space program would soon not need them, and that their best hope of continued employment was to set up their own electronics firm. They were intrigued with what could be done with the latest generation of chips, which uniquely combined falling prices with increasing power. A friend of a friend helped them raise money in San Antonio, with the stipulation that the start-up be located there. (He saw no reason to leave.) They incorporated in July of 1968 under the name Computer Terminal Corp. (CTC), and were shipping their first product for revenue in August 1969.

That first product was what was then called a "glass teletype," an electronic plug-compatible replacement for the noisy, unreliable electro-mechanical teletype (or teleprinter) machines then used as computer terminals. We would call it a "dumb tube," being a computer terminal with no local intelligence. They named it the Datapoint 3300, as it was supposed to be a hundred times better than the Model 33 Teletype.

Even before it shipped they began working on the follow-up product, revealing to select individuals that the Datapoint 3300 was just something to get the company started. Their real intent was to make a desktop computer, which they called the Datapoint 2200. It was to have the same desktop footprint as an IBM Selectric typewriter, so that it would fit into an office setting—but that also made it very crowded inside the box. They hired engineer Vic Poor, who spent the 1969 Thanksgiving holiday with several associates designing a stripped-down instruction set for the computer they foresaw.

A few weeks later, during the Christmas season, Poor visited a fellow startup in California, chip-maker Intel, that had been founded two weeks after CTC. CTC used a lot of Intel's latest memory chips (slow shift registers, rather than later, faster RAM chips) for the Datapoint 3300, and he was checking order status. And he was aware of how packed the internals of the new Datapoint 2200 were turning out to be, so he asked about the possibility of Intel making a custom chip that would incorporate multiple processor functions. Poor and the Intel engineer he talked to, Stan Mazor, disagree about who suggested putting the whole processor on one chip, but that was the project that Intel soon agreed to undertake with CTC. Putting all the processor functions on one chip would save a full circuit board. Work on the chip (initially called the 1201) began at Intel in March 1970. Not knowing how long Intel would take, CTC wisely proceeded with a version of the Datapoint 2200 with a full-board processor.

Development of the 1201 chip at Intel proceeded into summer—when it was halted because CTC had stopped paying its bills. Indeed, the firm spent its first few years careening from one financial crisis to another. IBM set the stage in the computer industry by leasing rather than selling hardware, so all other computer firms had to do the same. Consequently, revenue from a sale took three years to dribble in. That was fine for well-funded IBM but catastrophic for smaller firms.

Despite everything, CTC managed to unveil the Datapoint 2200 in November 1970. Its programming was in terms of eight-bit bytes, but internally it operated with a one-bit data path. Its speed was 125,000 cycles per second. (Today's desktop machines have 64-bit bit data paths with speeds topping out at 4 billion cycles per second.) It could address about 8,000 bytes of internal storage. (The minimum today is usually 4 billion bytes.) Mass storage was on two cassette tape drives holding about 130,000 bytes each. (Today, desktop hard drives with a trillion bytes are becoming common.) Outwardly, the most striking difference from modern machines was that the (text-only) screen was only 12 lines high, to mimic the aspect of an IBM punch card. The lower height also made the machine less intimidating to office workers accustomed to typewriters.

The first customer installation was at the Pillsbury headquarters in Minneapolis on April 7, 1971. Although CTC's engineers assumed the buyers would be interested in using the Datapoint 2200 for terminal emulation and other generic tasks involving canned programs, the users instead embraced it as a cheap, general purpose computer, often writing their own programs.

Meanwhile, back at Intel, a Japanese client expressed interest in the 1201 chip, and development resumed in early 1971.

That Intel chip seems to have been forgotten back at CTC, which immediately began development of the Datapoint 2200 Version II, which could support a hard drive plus an astronomical 16,000 bytes of memory. Weirdly, in June 1971 Texas Instruments announced that it had developed a single-chip version of the Datapoint 2200 processor, implying it would be used in Version II. But when the first sample was delivered, CTC's engineer could not make it work. Texas Instruments then scrapped the whole project, not to mention the corporate division that produced the chip, killing their chance to become the founder of the microcomputer revolution.

CTC answered with an even bigger blunder soon afterward, during the autumn of 1971, when Intel finally delivered samples of the 1201 chip. It emulated the processor of the original Datapoint 2200, although with a true eight-bit data path. However, CTC was by then developing the more powerful Datapoint 2200 Version II, and was uninterested in new circuitry for the original version. So it was agreed: CTC would keep its money, and Intel would keep the chip and the intellectual property it represented.

But what the California-centric historians dwell on was the announcement soon afterward (on November 15, 1971) of the Intel 4004 processor chip, usually hailing it as the first computer chip. Actually, with a mere 640 bytes of memory and a four-bit data path, it could not have been used for a computer, and never was. (It had been offered to Poor when he visited Intel during Christmas 1969, but he turned it down.) The 4004 was Intel's response to a Japanese vendor that wanted to make a scientific calculator, and by using a processor with a stored program they could cut the number of chips from a dozen to four. The project was green-lighted in September 1969 but when an engineer from the Japanese firm showed up at Intel in early April 1970 almost nothing had been done, due to a shortage of chip designers. He got things going again, but real work was already under way on the Datapoint project. It would have come out first had it not been put on ice for six months when summer came.

The long-delayed Datapoint processor chip was finally put in the Intel catalog in April 1972. It was renamed the 8008, as its data path was double that of the previous 4004, and some histories state that it was an extension of the 4004. As the previous paragraph implies, the two had nothing in common.

Sales of the 8008 were good enough to justify further development, and the next generation 8080 (which was 10 times faster and could use 64,000 bytes of RAM) came out in April 1974. It was this chip, plus competitors that started coming out after about six months, that sparked the revolution.

The competitors began falling away after the IBM PC came out in August 1981. It was based on the 8088, a stripped-down version of the 8086, which was an expanded version of the 8080. Cheap PCs began flooding the market, and these machines grew cheaper yet more powerful as each enhanced generation of processor chips came out. Today, computers that use them are referred to as x86 machines and are ubiquitous in modern offices—even Apple machines now use x86 processors.

That means that any desktop machine you can point to is a direct descendent of the original Datapoint 2200.

The irony is that CTC (renamed Datapoint Corp. in late 1972) not only did not profit from the success of its creation, but was destroyed by it. Thanks to the parting agreement between Intel and CTC in 1971, the Texans got no royalties from the technology they created. Meanwhile, prices of the new PCs were a third that of the previous desktop machines (including Datapoint's). To make things worse, an accounting scandal caused Datapoint's stock price to collapse in 1982, leading to a takeover by a Wall Street raider who said he thought it would be fun to run a computer company.

He was wrong, and Datapoint never recovered, although dissolution was staved off until 2000.

The puzzled questions died away, and there was no one left to challenge the Silicon Valley creation myth. The Datapoint 2200 came out about seven years before the commonly accepted start of the microcomputer revolution in 1977, but has been written out of the story.

BOOKS, MOVIES, AND COMPUTERS

Anyone writing anything that purports to be about the future runs the risk of four different scenarios:

1. You'll be correct, but your predictions are initially shrugged off as bizarre or meaningless, offering only entertainment value, until such time as previously unconnected circumstances suddenly come together and it's clear that your predictions have come true. Then there'll be a few remarks about the curious fact that you were right. You might even show up in a book like this one. Then your predictions will be shrugged off again and life will go on.

2. People will want you to be correct, and invest great meaning in your words. Of course, you won't be correct, and you'll dash the hopes of followers you never knew you had. But the fact that they clung to you means you successfully articulated what they were going to want, and that's a powerful form of prediction.

3. People will want you to be correct, and invest great effort in making it so, leaving a wide swath of destruction as they do so. Your followers never get it through their heads that you were being descriptive, not prescriptive, or that the scope of your predictions were never as cosmic as they seemed to think.

4. You'll be utterly incorrect, and nothing like your predictions will ever take place. But tomorrow never comes, so if you wrote your predictions in a way that catches the public imagination people will continue talking about them indefinitely—or at least until the next fad strikes. This is especially true if you were predicting some kind of moral, political, financial, cultural, climatic, or ecological apocalypse, and/or complaining about "what's wrong with kids these days."

This section examines several examples of #1, which seem to be, historically, under-appreciated, plus one of #2, and another that sort of merges #1 and #2.

As for #3, there have been plenty of them, often with avid promoters, and they generally lack entertainment value. So we'll do without. As for #4, there's a new crop of them every year, predicting the doom of anything and everything up to and including the publishing industry itself. In fact, you can take this as a prediction of their upcoming predictions. Enough said.

And by now it should obvious that we have been dancing around the main point of this section, that there have been books or movies that successfully predicted the future (more or less). Under a strictly rational construction of reality, that's not possible. But it has happened. How?

Answering that question would involve predicting what the next sections are going to say. Read on.

28
Pearl Harbor Rehearsal

Some of the results of the Japanese surprise attack on Pearl Harbor, which opened the Pacific War. The war was prophesized in some detail in a book written 16 years earlier, although the author was not totally accurate—he assumed, for instance, that the opening surprise attack would hit the Panama Canal. Public domain image from Wikimedia Commons.

Any book written about the Pacific War of 1941–45 would have to mention the surprise attack that began it all, the Japanese capture of Guam and the Philippines, Japanese suicide attacks, the American island-hopping campaign, the re-conquest of the Philippines and Guam, the commerce raiding, the savage surface actions, and the aerial attacks on Japanese cities that led to the collapse of that island nation.

The Great Pacific War by Hector C. Bywater covers all that. The problem is that it was written in 1925, 16 years before Pearl Harbor.

Bywater was a British naval writer who also reported for American newspapers and at times worked for British intelligence. His book foresaw Japan quickly overrunning the Western Pacific but proving unable to stave off a methodical American counter-offensive. Japanese technology is as good as American technology, and Japanese personnel are actually better trained, but the Americans are able to apply more resources where they are needed.

But Bywater's war ran from 1931 to 1933, not 1941 to 1945. Instead of the conflict being part of a global war, it stems from a trade dispute involving China, and neither side has any allies. There is some fighting in Manchuria and northern China, but the rest of East Asia is not involved. Other discontinuities:

- The opening surprise move is a suicide attack on the Panama Canal with an exploding freighter, closing the seaway for six months. *The real opening move was the infamous Pearl Harbor attack. Despite losses, the bases there remained operational.*

- The Japanese take Guam only on the second attempt, the first having been bloodily repulsed. *In reality, it was the tiny garrison at Wake Island that defeated the initial landing force, but fell to the second attempt. Guam fell on the first attempt.*

- The Americans attack the Bonin Islands at Chichi Jima, for its harbor. *In reality they invaded Iwo Jima, farther south, for its air fields.*

- The move against the Bonins is part of an "immediate counter-attack" strategy early in the war, and is unsuccessful. *In reality the invasion was late in the war, part of an island-hopping strategy, and was successful, albeit bloody.*

- After the Bonins failure the Americans launch an island-hopping campaign through the Caroline and Marshall islands. *Island hopping was adopted without ado, presumably by men who read the book, but they followed several vectors.*

- The Japanese probe the storm-wracked Aleutians but don't bother to invade. *They should have stuck to the book.*

- Truk lagoon is taken by the Americans. *The Japanese would build a substantial naval base there, which the Americans bypassed.*

- Anguar in the "Pelew" (Palau) island group is taken without difficulty by the Americans, who want its harbor. *There was bloody fighting there, and more especially at nearby Peleliu, which was taken for its airfield.*

- The Japanese fleet is crippled in the decisive Battle of Yap Island. *That was about a thousand miles east of where it was crippled in the Battle of the Philippines Sea.*
- Poison gas is used, even against ships and airplanes. *Both sides carried gas equipment, but gas saw no real use.*
- Both sides have aircraft carriers, but the planes are too small to carry devastating bombs and have only limited success when attacking large enemy warships that are in the habit of shooting back. They are more useful for scouting and artillery spotting, although they can be decisive in that role. *This would have been the case in 1925 when the book was written, and perhaps in 1931, when the story was supposed to take place, but was no longer the case in 1941.*
- The Americans make good use of decoy ships to ambush the Japanese. *They used code-breaking to enable ambushes. Improved aerial reconnaissance made decoy ships useless.*
- Zeppelins are used by the Americans for oceanic scouting. *The U.S. Navy stopped operating them in 1935 after its last one crashed off California. Blimps were still used for off-shore patrols.*
- Japanese inhabitants of Oahu stage an unsuccessful insurrection. *One was feared.*
- Bywater names commanders on both sides, but they were all fictional. *He names ships on both sides, too, and many were real. Chillingly, some of them showed up in the real war.*
- Speaking of named ships, he postulates that the Japanese would convert the carrier *Akagi* to a battle-cruiser after they decide they have enough carriers. *In reality they later converted cruisers to carriers, and the Akagi, as a carrier, was at Pearl Harbor, and was sunk at Midway.*
- The campaign against Japanese merchant shipping takes place in the Atlantic, involves surface raiders rather than submarines, and the Japanese use their superior cruisers to get the upper hand. *The real campaign involved submarines in the Pacific, and the Japanese were routed.*
- The Japanese military follows humane policies and avoids war crimes, to avoid alienating neutrals. *Sadly, this was not the case.*

■ The culminating air raids involve dropping only propaganda leaflets on Japanese cities, which trigger enough popular unrest to bring down the government. *Sadly, this was not the case.*

But the main thrust is prophetic: seeking revenge for surprise attack, the U.S forces use island-hopping to penetrate Japan's defense perimeter of island bases to bring the war to the Home Islands.

Did Bywater have foreknowledge? In one sense, yes, clearly he did. He was an expert on naval affairs who understood the interaction of technology, geography, and national policy. He was alarmed by the naval arms race that Japan and America were pursuing in the 1920s, and the book demonstrates that the logical outcome would be a Pacific war, and the results would be painful for both parties. Those who thought the size of the Pacific precluded war, or that the Americans could simply counterattack and immediately crush the Japanese, or that the Japanese were too backward and/or near-sighted to be dangerous, were all wrong. His warnings were confirmed on all counts.

But if he had true foreknowledge he would have foreseen more powerful airplanes, radar, death marches, massed carrier raids, fleets of strategic bombers, fire bombings, concentration camps, genocide, nations enslaved by demonic madmen, and nuclear weapons.

Or, perhaps he did—one report hints that his death in London in August 1940 was from alcoholism.

But the bigger question is whether Isoroku Yamamoto read the book. He was a Japanese naval attaché (that is, a legal, mutually acknowledged spy) in the United States during the 1920s and at one point attended Harvard. More to the point, he later rose to command the Japanese fleet and masterminded the Pearl Harbor attack and Japan's early triumphs in the war—triumphs that pretty much followed the book.

The answer: Absolutely Yamamoto read the book, especially the first half with the easy Japanese victories. He is known to have lectured about it at a training school, and made of point of meeting Bywater in 1934, spending an evening with him at a naval conference.

After things soured for Japan, after the defeats at Midway, Coral Sea, and Guadalcanal, one wonders if he got the book out and started reading ahead. He would have had ample time to do it while flying to outposts for inspection visits, such as the one from Rabaul to the Bougainville area in April 1943. We'll never know—he died on that trip, after being intercepted by long-range American fighters.

That was not in the book.

29
The Apollo Script

Inside their aluminum space capsule, Jules Verne's three fictional astronauts experience free-fall after being launched towards the moon, 103 years before three real astronauts would make the journey in an aluminum space capsule. NASA/courtesy of nasaimages.org.

A three-man crew is launched into space from Florida and circles the moon before returning to Earth, splashing down in the ocean. The impetus for the project—which becomes a focus of national pride—is a challenge issued by a national leader, and a desire to make creative use of the nation's military industrial complex. Texas vied to be the launching site.

If you wanted to hit the high points of the U.S. space program through the 1968 Apollo 8 mission (discounting the earlier Mercury and Gemini programs as mere pilot projects), the previous paragraph probably suffices. But actually, it more accurately sums up the plot of the novel *From the Earth to the Moon*, written (in French) by Jules Verne in 1865. In other words, 103 years earlier.

Verne, of course, was a science fiction author famous for making predictions about technology that came true. Living from 1828 to 1905, his predictions included (in some form, sometimes arguably) electricity, cars, nuclear submarines, air conditioners, calculators and computers, the Internet, mutually assured destruction, skyscrapers, neurotic career women, armies that are difficult to enlist in, bullet trains, execution with the electric chair, fax machines, technological advances at the expense of cultural impoverishment, television, climate change, and the rebuilding of the Louvre museum in Paris with a geometric motif.

But frankly, such predictions (aside from that thing about the Louvre) were extensions (albeit sometimes extreme ones) of technology, gadgets, or trends that were not unknown in his day. On a hot day anyone who knew about adiabatic cooling could dream up an air conditioner. Someone who had heard of the advantages of internal combustion over external combustion (i.e., steam power) and was repelled by what horses do to roads, could dream up an automobile. In Verne's day the world was already wired for the telegraph, so adding computers produces the Internet. And so on. Practical implementation might consume decades, but that was not his problem.

But a space program to circumnavigate the moon as an expression of national prestige was not an extension of anything that you can point to in the 19th century. Yes, they sent out explorers into unknown territory—but that was to make maps, whose utility was obvious. Going to the moon did not have obvious utility. (Considering the lack of follow-up to the Apollo program, there is evidently still some debate about that.)

The big difference between Verne's story and the Apollo program is that Verne used a cannon rather than rockets, and his was literally a one-shot program. Beyond that, the closer you look at the parallels between Verne's story and the Apollo program, the more startling they appear.

Basically, Verne's story involves the employment of artillerists left over from the Civil War, and the project is spurred on by a bet made by an industrialist. The Apollo program involved resources redeployed from the Cold War, and was spurred on by a commitment by President Kennedy, shortly before his assassination, that the U.S. must get to the moon before the end of the 1960s (and thus crush the Soviet Union in the space race they had recently sparked).

Other evocative parallels:

- Verne's cannon was called the Columbiad while the Apollo 8 command module was called *Columbia*.
- Texas and Florida vied to be the launch site—in both the book and in reality. Verne's fictional cannon was built about 120 miles from the real Apollo launch site. In reality, Texas got the control center in Houston as a condolence prize.
- The project sparked a firestorm of press coverage, in both the Verne story and the Apollo program.
- The Apollo program included the construction of a tracking network. Verne's story included a custom-made tracking telescope.
- Both the Verne and the Apollo space capsules were made out of aluminum, and were expensive to make.
- Both carried three men.
- Verne's space capsule weighed about 9.5 tons, whereas the Apollo capsule weighed about 13 tons.
- Vast numbers of tourists gathered to watch the launch, in both cases.
- Both Verne's capsule and *Apollo 8* were launched in December and took several days to get to the moon.
- Both orbited the moon and then returned to Earth. Apollo 8 did this on purpose, whereas Verne's astronauts did it after the retrorockets intended for a lunar landing proved inadequate. (The fate of Verne's capsule, after launch, was covered in a sequel written in 1870 titled *Around the Moon*.)
- *Apollo 8* landed in the Pacific several hundred miles south of Johnston Atoll and was picked up by a U.S. Navy vessel. Verne's capsule landed in the Pacific several hundred miles off the coast of Mexico and was likewise picked up by a U.S. Navy vessel.
- Verne's program was depicted as costing $5.4 million in 1865. That has been calculated as the equivalent of $12.1 billion in 1969. Up to then, the Apollo program is reported to have cost $14.4 billion. So, from the distance of a century, Verne was 84-percent accurate. Like many amateur project managers, perhaps he didn't allow enough for managerial overhead.

Besides the absence of electronics in the 1865 version, the biggest point of departure between the two stories is also the simplest: the Apollo program did take place, and achieved its goal of manned lunar spaceflight. On the other hand, Verne's space program never took place, and if something like it had been attempted the result would not have been manned lunar space-flight. With the technology of 1865 they might have been able to build and fire a huge gun (described as being 900 feet long with a 9-foot bore, buried vertically in the ground) with the proper force and in the proper direction. But the astronauts would not have survived the acceleration of being shot out of a cannon. In fact, Verne had naysayers in the novel pointing this out. Perhaps Verne had a sinking feeling that someone might attempt the project.

And he was correct. But in the 1960s they had technology (rockets) that could put a person into space with survivable acceleration (that is, a few Gs, rather than thousands). Other issues involving engineering and orbital dynamics remained the same, however, and were subject to the same general solution. And so things like capsule size and mission duration resemble each other.

Verne's story was obviously a reverse anachronism of the second kind—an item that starts out being from the future, until it is perceived as belonging to the present. One wonders if, thousands of years from now, scholars will have trouble distinguishing the Verne from the Apollo version of events. Both may seem equally improbable.

And indeed, how can we explain it today? The Apollo program represented such a unique combination of circumstances that foreseeing it a century in advance is asking a lot.

If Verne had genuine foreknowledge, his story would have relied on rockets instead of a cannon. But the results would probably have been less acceptable to his readers, who knew only black powder rockets that were weak, uncontrollable, and predisposed to explode. To preserve the book's commercial appeal he might have used a cannon anyway, with some mention of a shock absorber in the space capsule that was supposed to make the launch survivable. (And that is exactly what the book does.)

And if he did have genuine foreknowledge, surely it would have showed up in his other 53 novels. And, as mentioned, it sort of does, but in an incomplete, flawed fashion, indicating that he was projecting existing trends.

If you're in the mood for irrational explanations, perhaps the moon program had such profound impact on the collective psyche that someone could unconsciously pick up its reverberations even a century in advance. When Verne expressed what he "heard" he translated it into 1865 terms.

Or maybe he was just a Frenchman saying that Americans are willing to go to the moon for national prestige.

He got that right.

30
20th Century "Foretold"

Edward Bellamy, whose predictions about utopian conditions in the year 2000 entranced countless readers in the latter part of the 19th century. He was right only where he would probably have preferred to be wrong. Public domain image from Wikimedia Commons.

Someone who fell into a trance in the gritty, tumultuous world of 1887 and awoke in the year 2000 would find himself in an aesthetically pleasing socialist utopia where war and crime had been eradicated. That's what the novel *Looking Backward: 2000–1887*, written by Edward Bellamy in 1888, would have us believe. Science fiction? Sort of. Really bad prognosticating? Definitely. Some kind of reverse anachronism? Not really—it's more of a cultural artifact, but one that speaks more to us today than we might like to admit.

Bellamy was a lawyer and writer who lived from 1850 to 1898. The book must have spoken to the yearnings of a lot of people in the latter half of the 19th century, as it was the third-ranking best seller of the era, after *Uncle Tom's Cabin* and *Ben-Hur*. There's no other explanation for its appeal, as the plot is bland, the prose stiff and rambling, and the action consists mostly of the awakened hero having long conversations with his host, who explains the flawless functioning of Bellamy's fictional 20th century's industrial economy while dissecting and dismissing as uniformly reprehensible the cultural norms of 1887. The hero also goes shopping, and to dinner at a communal dining hall, and eventually decides he likes the host's daughter—and that's about it

Through it all, the book lays out (and then beats to death with preachy prose) a number of predictions, ranging in scope from colossal to trivial:

- The economy of 1887 was too inefficient to satisfy the demands of organized labor for a better life, and there was no way it ever could. *In reality, thanks to subsequent technological innovations, affluence has become widely attainable and obesity has reached epidemic proportions.*

- The monopolistic business practices that were trampling competition in 1887 would triumph. *In reality, the Sherman Anti-Trust Act was passed, two years after the book was written, for the express purpose of thwarting monopolistic practices, and generally worked as intended. Throughout the decades the American Tobacco Co., Standard Oil, National Cash Register, IBM, and Microsoft have all felt the wrath of Gen. Sherman's younger brother.*

- All the rampant monopolies were then allowed to congeal into one huge enterprise that was then absorbed by the government, effortlessly effecting a bloodless and successful social revolution, leaving the government as the sole (and benevolent) employer. *Some countries tried this, and the revolutions were bloody, massively disruptive, and ultimately unsuccessful.*

- In the new order everyone gets paid the same salary for their work, except harder jobs have shorter work hours. *Forty-hour workweeks have become standard since 1887. There is usually a statutory minimum wage.*

- The labor force is organized like an army, with induction at 21, partial retirement at 45, and full retirement at 55. *College graduates may enter the workforce around age 21, and retirement age varies—but is well beyond 55 in most non-medical cases.*

- There are no longer any wars, as hunger, cold, and nakedness have been accepted as the real enemies. *It's not polite to laugh at people's sincere beliefs.*

- Crime is treated as a medical problem. *There's some of that today.*
- Women get the same wage as men and can take as much maternity leave as they like. *We are not even close.*
- Freight is moved through large pneumatic tubes. *Later tinkering with the idea mostly underscored the practicality of trucks.*
- Women's fashions would get less elaborate. *Purely in terms of appearance, that's true.*
- Men's fashions would be largely the same. *They're at least recognizable.*
- Chimneys and the pervading smoky urban haze are forgotten. *That's effectively true.*
- Cultured speech had not changed much in 113 years. *I cannot with alacrity assent to that proposition. In some eras you have to use flowery language or be labeled a simpleton. 1887 may have been such an era, but 2000 was not.*
- Shop owners were turned into clerks in large stores. *Shopped at Wal-Mart recently?*
- Alarm clocks would play music. *We have plenty of that.*
- There's an a international organization like the United Nations, and it works. *There's a United Nations, but the word "work" requires some definition.*
- Literally everything is paid for through credit cards. *We're close.*
- Cost is determined by the labor content of an item. *Supply and demand still rule.*

Bellamy makes almost no predictions of a technological nature. Electricity is mentioned exactly once. The telephone is described primarily as a way of piping in music from live performances, and there is no mention of recorded performances, yet, in 1887 the phonograph had been known for about a decade. There is no mention of automobiles or any other form of mass transit. However, retractable roofs for sidewalks eliminate the need for umbrellas.

Obviously, Bellamy was not Jules Verne. Bellamy was interested in predicting (if not triggering) social progress, not technological progress. And what he defined as social progress suggested a glittering, refined refugee camp, with a cultural norm of military-like conformity, where people ate in communal dining halls, and where labor was a form of self-expression. In fact, you dignified labor by refusing to set a price on it.

In other words, the book was an elitist social prescription written by someone who had never been in the army, or sweated out a shift in a coal mile or a shipyard, or gotten up before dawn to tend the livestock.

Apparently, Bellamy (and presumably his many readers, some of whom set up political clubs in his name) yearned for the obvious benefits of an industrial economy, without all the unseemly, disquieting agitation and unpredictability that underpinned it. They wanted the price of both labor and commercial products to be set by "boards of sensible men" like themselves, rather than submit to the indignity of them being set by soulless economic mechanisms.

Alas, it has been discovered the hard way since 1888 that you can't have your cake and eat it too—putting prices on things might seem like a handy rationing mechanism, but the concept of price is not meaningful when divorced from an underlying economy. Yes, boards of sensible men can set prices, but they are doing so in a vacuum. The result is a sort of toy economy riddled with pockets of massive inefficiency, there being no obvious way to gauge efficiency in economic terms when the price of everything is arbitrary. In the end the edifice has to be propped up by coercion. In the Soviet Union the intermediate result was workers saying, "They pretend to pay us so we pretend to work." The long-term result was the total collapse and dissolution of the Soviet Union.

Meanwhile, the book implied an assumption that personal dignity has to be bestowed by some outside influence, which in a perfect world would involve participation in labor whose nature and conditions would be defined by a board of sensible men. The relationship of the individual to himself or herself is not even acknowledged.

That's par for garden-variety elitism, but Bellamy is particularly noteworthy by modern standards by his belief that big business and big government are not automatically bad things. They would grow and evolve and co-mingle and naturally create a nirvana thanks to the wise application of their unlimited economic-industrial-political authority. Bellamy probably saw no other way for his brave new world to arise—and there probably wasn't. But in the meantime the implication was that interested parties did not need to do anything except sit back and wait for wonderful things to happen.

Alas, his elitist prescription was competing with that of Karl Marx, which gave interested parties something to do (launch bloody revolutions) and the moral license to do it. Unsurprisingly, Marx won far more mindshare. Beyond bloodshed and economic ruin, one result was generations of righteous elitists preaching "Power to the people," meaning (somehow) themselves. "Power to the *correct* people," responded jaded cynics—at least, those residing outside the jurisdictions of the resulting elitist dictatorships dared say it, for otherwise the consequences could involve a mass grave. Bellamy, however, preached power to the bureaucrats, and no mass graves were dug in his name.

Today we see righteous elitists preaching the horror of government regulation—except in areas where they think regulation is needed. They seem quite attached to policed and maintained roads, inspected food, cholera-free tap water, safe and effective medication, and honest banks and stock brokers. Power to the *correct* bureaucrats, in other words.

So perhaps, in the end, Bellamy truly was a prophet.

31
The Internet in 1945

Artist's conception of Vannevar Bush's 1945 memex, with a scanner window on the left, dual display screens with controlling joysticks in the middle, and a keyboard on the right. Had they been able to build it, the user experience would have been nearly identical to that of today's World Wide Web. Drawing by Amanda Hernandez. Used with permission.

On your desk sits a visual display device with multiple windows, with a keyboard and special controls. It lets you browse through vast amounts of material, including encyclopedias especially adapted to this media. As you find material you like you can record the links to it, and even reuse those links in other material.

Of course, the preceding is a partial description of the way you use the Internet. Except that it isn't—it's a summary of a description of a knowledge worker's "enlarged intimate supplement to his memory," called a memex. Presidential science advisor Vannevar Bush (1890–1974) basically demanded its invention in a magazine article in 1945, as a way to keep up with the ever-increasing volume of scientific literature.

The article was titled "As We May Think" and appeared in the July 1945 issue of *The Atlantic Monthly*, a high-brow magazine for intellectuals. (It was later covered in the middle-brow *Life* Magazine with some beneficial editing, plus added artwork.) It's available online, and reading it with a Web browser can be a supremely eerie experience, as you gradually realize that the act of reading it in that mode fulfills its implied prophecies.

Of course, Bush didn't get everything right. Basically, he glossed over the technical details, assuming that some way would be found to make the machine do what he wanted, probably using advanced microfilm technology or thermionic tubes (that is, vacuum tubes). In fact, it would be done with the descendents of those tubes—transistors, billions of them on silicon chips. He foresaw the involvement of a network, but assumed it would be the post office.

A former MIT professor and cofounder of Raytheon, Bush was head of President Roosevelt's Office of Scientific Research and Development during World War II, and oversaw the crash development of a wide variety of leading-edge technologies, like radar, antibiotics, proximity fuses, jet planes, homing torpedoes, and that project they didn't tell Vice President Truman about until he became President Truman, code-named Manhattan. Keeping up with the literature on such divergent subjects must have been a prodigious task, and his 8,100-word article was basically a complaint about the inadequacies of the available tools.

About 2/3 through the article he began offering his answer, the memex (not to be confused with a later Scottish software firm of the same name). Outwardly it would be an ordinary desk, but on top would be slanting translucent screens, a keyboard, a "transparent platen" that acts as a scanner, and some buttons and levers. It would come with a preloaded library of books, journals, and magazines, presumably using future microfilm technology that he speculated about earlier in the article, which would let you store a million books within a desk. There would be a facility for adding notations to individual items. The user would then add his personal books, records, and communications to the memex's database.

Retrieval of any one item can be immediate, by punching in a code. Forward-back buttons let the user navigate through an item, and there is a special button to jump to an item's index. An item would be left on one screen while calling up another item on a second screen. The user would keep a log book of codes, typically under handy mnemonic names. Then the user would record the codes of items of a particular topic and string them together, in a process he called associative indexing.

Bush wanted his memex to use associative indexing on the assumption that such indexing matches the workings of the human mind—thinking about one topic calls up other topics associated with it. In the mind, the creation of trails between associated items is fast and complex, but transitory. But with the memex you could make a permanent record.

People would publish trails of associative items that would be useful for various purposes or within specific professions. Apparently, every memex is assumed to have the same bulk contents, and presumably gets the same periodic updates through the mail. The article states that microfilmed material could be mailed cheaply but otherwise does not get specific. Publication would be through a microfilm reproducer.

In later writings he speculated that, in the future, professional and scientific journals would no longer be published on paper, but as memex database updates, possibly delivered via fax.

He also called for speech recognition as an input method, and speculated on the possibility of a direct brain interface.

So let's compare Bush's vision to the reality of Internet use six-plus decades later:

- Microfilm storage. *Electronic storage.*
- Storage of personal correspondence and records in a desk device. *Storage of personal correspondence and records in a desktop device.*
- Slanting translucent screens. *Computer displays.*
- Multiple display windows. *Multiple display windows.*
- Keyboards. *Keyboards.*
- Transparent platen. *Scanner.*
- Back/forward buttons. *Back/forward screen icons.*
- Mnemonic address codes. *URLs.*
- Associative trails. *Hypertext.*
- Logs of associative trails. *Browser favorites.*
- Published associative trails. *Wikis, news portals, linked blogs.*
- Index page access via dedicated buttons. *Homepage access via dedicated buttons.*
- Ability to add notations to data. *Typically you can edit only your own material online.*
- Access to a million books. *Access to millions (billions?) of book equivalents.*
- Data distribution by mail. *Data distribution by e-mail.*

- Microfilm reproducers. *Printers, e-mail, Web pages.*
- Professional and scientific publication via memex database updates. *Professional and scientific publication via Websites.*
- Speech recognition. *Speech recognition—it's an unadvertised feature in later versions of Microsoft Windows.*
- Direct mind input. *Not really. (People keep working on this, but the suspicion is that if we ever do get it, it will require so much concentration and training that the end result will be about the same as typing.)*

The present-day Web entity that does not show up in Bush's article is the search engine—all the "intelligence" in the memex would stem from the user's keeping of a log book. The associative indexes would have been derived from the user's perception and judgment. In other words, they would have to have been be manually generated, based on at least cursory personal examination of targeted material, presumably identified through traditional subject indexes. Had the idea of a search engine been suggested to Bush it might not have thrilled him—being based on simple word matching, most search engines provide results that are associative only by accident. It is up to the users to blaze a trail through the resulting thicket of raw material, using their perception and judgment. And that's exactly what Bush expected users to do with the memex. However, he might have appreciated the search engine as a self-generating, albeit primitive index.

As an example of what could be done with a memex, he describes a hypothetical user musing about the history of the bow and arrow, and looking into the fact that the English never adopted the Turkish short bow, even though it obviously outranged their longbows during the Crusades. The hypothetical memex user assembles an associative trail that delves deeply into the matter, even to textbooks on elasticity. He wraps it up by appending his own analysis. Later he passes it on to a friend when they get into a discussion about people's resistance to innovation (a subject probably dear to Bush's heart). The hypothetical memex user concludes that the medieval British were greatly at fault for succumbing to cultural inertia by not adopting Turkish bow technology.

And here we get to the fact that his memex was never built. It needed agile, high-speed, high-density microfilm with electronic control for highly selective, high-speed retrieval, and that was never practical. Oddly enough, putting a million books in a desk did turn out to be possible—assuming an average of 60,000 words each, with no artwork, it could be done with fewer than a hundred DVDs. The issue would be designing a DVD jukebox that would fit in a desk.

The World Wide Web arose instead. It has features that closely resemble the memex, but that is probably because its collective designers were responding to the same pressures that Bush was responding to. Although the memex is clearly a reverse anachronism, there is no reason to assume that Bush had any psychic foreknowledge, or was some kind of time traveler (although UFO researchers/conspiracy advocates link him to secret government UFO research and/or a secret committee running the country under the direct control of extraterrestrials.)

Anyway, if Bush was not firmly rooted in 1945 he would not have used a hypothetical memex search about the failure of the English to adopt the Turkish bow and cite it as an example of cultural inertia. Querying a real 21st-century search engine on the real Web with the phrase "Turkish bow construction" would have pointed him to material that mentioned that Turkish bows required copious amounts of exotic glue made from the mouth parts of Danube River sturgeon. The glue absorbed moisture so readily that the bows were non-functional in humidity over 70 percent, and were typically stored in heated containers.

In other words, they would have been useless in the wet weather of foggy old England, and the medieval English were better off sticking to their longbows—something they probably figured out on their own.

A military technology decision—Vannevar Bush knew about those.

32
Wag the Dog

President Bill Clinton and White House intern Monica Lewinsky, whose entanglement during a Balkans crisis was eerily foretold by the movie Wag the Dog. *Public domain images from Wikimedia Commons.*

The president of the United States, finding himself involved in a sex scandal, gets America involved in military operations in Albania. Obviously, we're talking about:

a. The plot of the 97-minute R-rated Hollywood movie *Wag the Dog*, released in December 1997 by New Line Cinema.

b. Outcome of the Bill Clinton–Monica Lewinsky sex scandal that erupted in January 1998, during which the United States responded to the genocide crisis in Kosovo by sending troops to join a peace-keeping coalition operating out of neighboring Albania.

c. Both of the above.

The answer is "both." The entire Clinton-Lewinski-Albania affair developed along lines eerily similar to the plot of the movie, and it began developing almost as soon as the movie reached the theaters. Those who wonder if the passage of time is an illusion were given additional evidence that it is.

Those who wonder if life imitates art could see that, yet again, things would go much smoother if it did, because fictional plots have to make sense.

As for the movie, it postulates that the president, running for reelection, is accused of molesting a teenage girl in the White House. Did he? We never learn—that's not the issue. The issue is that news of the accusation is about to break 11 days before the election, and a fixer is brought in to keep the country distracted during that interval. He starts leaking rumors of a crisis with Albania involving anti-American terrorists operating from there. He teams with a Hollywood producer to make anti-Albanian terrorist propaganda footage and sappy war songs. Things go well for a few days, but then the president abruptly declares victory and ends the fictional war. Undaunted, the team cooks up information about an American soldier left behind within terrorists lines inside Albania, trying to send encouraging messages to his mother. They manufacture his rescue. Their stand-in for the soldier turns out to be a military prison inmate who's been put away for rape, but they are prepared to deal with that problem, mostly with the help of anti-psychotic medication. But then their plane goes down in a storm while on their way to stage the fake hero's grand return to the United States after his fake rescue, and he runs off and gets killed while molesting a farmer's daughter. The team find he's as useful dead as alive and the charade continues. But then the movie producer becomes outraged that pundits are crediting the president's now successful reelection campaign to a series of lame TV commercials created by someone else. The producer demands public credit for his behind-the-curtains management of the Albanian "crisis," and as a result soon dies of a "sudden, massive heart attack" while tanning by his pool—despite the foggy, winter weather.

The all-star cast doubtless helped the film make a profit despite the absence of car chases and an approach to humor that was probably too low-key and cerebral for the mass market. The best line is probably the fixer's response to a CIA executive who complains that the agency's spy satellites can't find any evidence of military operations in Albania: "Then what use are they?" And of course, there's the reminder that all combat takes place at night, in the rain, at the intersection of four map sections.

The theatrical circuit was pretty much done with the film by the end of January 1998. The cast and crew had gone on to other projects. The audience had absorbed the movie's message that perceptions trump reality in politics, that perceptions can be manufactured cheaply—and that an Albanian crisis could be helpful during a presidential sex scandal.

And then life began imitating art—sloppily. In the last week of January allegations surfaced of a relationship between then President Bill Clinton and Monica Lewinsky, who had been a White House intern. Lewinsky had been transferred to the Pentagon, but gossiped about her relationship with Clinton during phone conversations with a friend, who recorded those conversations. Clinton began issuing forceful denials, which continued through the summer of 1998.

At the same time, the long-standing ethnic crisis in Kosovo began to heat up. Kosovo is a province in what was once Yugoslavia that lies across the border from Albania, and ethnic Albanians are heavily represented in its population. After the breakup of Yugoslavia, Kosovo ended up in a region dominated by the Serbs, and friction there between the Serbs and ethnic Albanians had risen to the point of genocide.

During 1998 hundreds of thousands of ethnic Albanians fled across the border to Albania, and others just hid in the woods, as reprisals and counter-reprisals continued between armed Serbs and ethnic Albanians in Kosovo. The United States joined various Western initiatives and sanctions intended to pressure the Serbs into a settlement.

Finally, on August 17, 1998, Clinton finally admitted to an "improper physical relationship" with Lewinski. However, he stood by his previous denials of a sexual relationship, saying that the exact nature of the physical relationship did not fit the given definition of a sexual relationship. Anyway, he did not "contact" her; she "contacted" him—no one bought this.

Back in Kosovo, Western powers managed to get both sides to a peace conference in Rambouillet, outside Paris, in early 1999. When these talks collapsed in March 1999 NATO raised the heat and began bombing Serbian forces, who finally backed down in June. Kosovo was then occupied by NATO peace-keepers, and rebuilding began.

Back in Washington, Clinton was impeached by the House of Representatives on December 19, 1998, on charges of perjury and obstruction of justice related to the sex scandal. The vote was mostly along party lines and it was only the second impeachment of an American president (the first occurring in 1868). The case was then tried in the Senate, as required by the U.S. Constitution, but the vote in February 1999 fell well short of the two-thirds needed for conviction and removal. (In 1868 conviction failed by one vote.)

The big difference between the movie and the subsequent reality is that, in the real world, the war actually happened. In the movie, the war was complete fiction, created to draw attention from a sex scandal, and had no existence outside the scandal. In the real world, ethnic tensions existed in Kosovo before Clinton and Lewinsky ever met, and continued for months after Clinton admitted to improprieties. Although Clinton might have reacted differently to the Kosovo crisis if he had not been in the middle of a sex scandal, it's hard to see how the outcome in Kosovo would have been much different.

Other differences:

- In the movie, the White House was the instigator and only participant in the Albanian crisis. (The Albanians were as surprised as anyone to read news of the crisis.) *In the real world, a multinational military coalition showed up, operating out of Albania. There was plenty of propaganda in play, as both the Serbians and the ethnic Albanians tried to claim the moral high ground.*

- In the movie, the girl was 15. *In the real world, Lewinsky was 22 years of age. when the relationship began. Clinton was 49 years old, so the relationship was well short of the traditional "half his age plus 7 years." Evidently this was more of a case of "a bad girl for fun and a good girl for courting."*

- Two people lose their lives in the movie. *The toll in the real world crisis ran to about 12,000.*

- Events took 11 days to play out in the movie. *In the real world, they limped on for more than a year.*

- The fictional president managed to shrug off the scandal. *Clinton was impeached, but easily survived the resulting trial in the senate. However, his party lost its grip on the next presidential election due to what pundits called "Clinton fatigue," leading to the unlikely ascendency of the ill-starred George W. Bush.*

But the ultimate lesson of the movie probably comes in the last seconds, when there is a news report of violence in Albania—and then the movie ends without letting the audience know if the report is supposed to be real, or just another chapter in the fictional crisis. And, in the real world, we are unequipped to know, from one report, if we are seeing fantasy or reality. Repeated, similar reports might be an indication that there is some reality behind the reports—or that someone is putting a lot of effort into maintaining the façade.

In other words, there might be a reality out there, someplace, but we always have to question whether we are really in touch with it.

Meanwhile, we can always go to the movies.

PRE-MODERN DEPICTIONS OF UFOS

Of course, Earth is constantly visited by benevolent star-traveling extra-terrestrials. Evidence of this can be glimpsed in the sky in the form of UFOs. Only constant government repression keeps this transcendent truth from being appreciated by the public. It's only natural that depictions of UFOs should show up occasionally in pre-modern artwork, because they're up there in the sky for any artist to see, and because the government wasn't as powerful back then.

And if you accept the previous paragraph without blinking you should skip ahead to Chapter 33. (Do read it though. Seriously.)

As for everyone else: Certain matters boil down to faith. For instance, you have to believe that the person you are talking to now is the same person you were talking to before you blinked. Yet, this is impossible to prove. Yes, it's simpler to assume that the person is the same, but simple assumptions are not always correct. They say the ceiling light glows brightly because by flicking the wall switch you connect its luminous bulb to a vast network of power generating stations and transmission networks—a mind-boggling assumption. Really, it sounds like a fairy tale told to children. Surely it's simpler and more logical to assume that the ceiling light is a luminous fruit that is excited by the manipulation of the wall switch.

Off on another tangent, you probably work under the assumption that the contents of your morning newspaper (or digital newsfeed) are based on some freestanding, generally agreed reality. The opinions voiced in its pages may not always mimic your own, and you may console yourself about that with various conspiracy theories. But if you tracked down the people and places mentioned in the news you would nevertheless expect to find that they did exist, and that the reports about them reflected (albeit dimly) some real event. Yet, there have been times and places (especially Stalin's Russia) where the contents of the newspapers were at times entirely invented, and slavishly reflected the ruler's vision of what ought to be happening, rather than the staff's discoveries of what was really going on.

So the belief that there are things in the sky that routinely go unreported is not all that extreme. If they are in the sky now, they could just as easily have been in the skies of Renaissance Italy, and so on, and any painter depicting the sky would include them. To believe they represent benevolent extraterrestrials requires an additional leap of faith, but who's to say it's not true? No one has disproved the theory—or ever will, because you can't prove a negative. It is subject to confirmation, such as a flying saucer landing on the White House lawn. If that does not happen today, it could still happen tomorrow, or the day after that, and so on.

In other words, don't waste your time expecting logic on this topic—but that's true for most topics, and often, the logic you do encounter is circular.

But now that we have finally introduced the concept of logic, it does seem odd that any beings who could traverse the universe would have any interest in us. If they were nonetheless interested in us, surely that interest would follow their agenda rather than ours, so it would seem benevolent only by accident.

That said, this section deals with depictions of objects in pre-modern artwork that fit modern preconceptions of what UFOs look like. As previously expounded, this is a field where faith outweighs logic. Those of the true faith will find that these images satisfyingly confirm their world view. Others will be interested to know that there are other explanations that may at times adhere closer to the generally accepted rules of logic. But remember, logic does not always lead to the correct answer.

Readers from both viewpoints should consider this: 3000 years from now Hollywoodology scholars may come across fragments of a collection labeled with the quaint lettering STAR WARS. They will be particularly intrigued by well-preserved scenes in which the characters are riding in a craft in orbital space, with no obvious acceleration, but are evidently experiencing gravity. The scene depicts hostile craft scooting back and forth in plain view. Yet, doing this in space at orbital velocities would involve deadly levels of acceleration. Meanwhile, the people depicted in the images keep firing projectiles at the hostile craft, typically missing. Everyone knows that in real space warfare you never get within sight of the enemy, and the low likelihood of missing is why they use so many decoys.

Various commentators pounce on these images, saying they are obviously intended to represent events inside a hyperspace field, where the laws of physics are subjective, and scenes like those depicted in the Star Wars material are entirely possible. Yet knowledge of hyperspace fields did not reach general circulation until the Post Coca-Cola Period, two full millennia after the time that the images in question were apparently created. Obviously, this is evidence that a benevolent race of star-traveling extraterrestrials visited Hollywood possibly as early as the Nixon Defenestration and imparted the information on, well, somebody.

Of course, anyone sitting in the audience in 1977 watching the movie *Star Wars* (somehow later renamed *Star Wars Episode IV: A New Hope*) would recognize the space combat scenes as being based on selected images of air combat (especially fighters versus bombers) in World War II, three decades earlier. Whether they were realistic was not an issue—a 1977 audience was conditioned by newsreels and war movies to accept them, and their depiction would not jar the audience members from their all-important suspension of disbelief. Plus the scenes offered some visual excitement to span slow periods in the narrative. Realistic space warfare (and for that matter, a lot of air warfare) would have been a visual bore.

They might be able to figure that out 3,000 years from now. And if they do, the art historians and the UFO believers will agree on one major point: The images are not there by accident. All the depictions are the result of a decision process. The UFO believers assume that the decision was to depict forbidden knowledge, hiding it in plain sight, so to speak. The art historians assume that the decision was to satisfy paying customers.

The same is true with the following material.

33
Madonna and UFO?

The "Natività di Gesù con San Giovannino," painted in the late 1400s, can be seen as illustrating the reality of flying saucers, or as illustrating the Renaissance's rich tradition of religious iconography. Public domain image from Wikimedia Commons.

There are UFO activists who refer to this painting as "the smoking gun." If flying saucers are real and not an artifact of modern media saturation on millions of imaginations, then they should have been in the skies all along. Throughout the centuries artists should have depicted them, if only by accident, long before the mass media started over-using flying saucers as a visual cliché in 1947.

And here we have "Natività di Gesù con San Giovannino" (Nativity of Jesus With the Infant John the Baptist) sometimes called "Madonna Col

Bambino E San Giovannino" (Madonna and Child with the Infant John the Baptist) by Sebastiano Mainardi (1460–1513), a 90 cm circular oil painting hanging in the Palazzo Vecchio in Florence, Italy. In the upper right, in the sky, is what appears to be a flying saucer—or at least some aerial object that's not a cloud. (At first glance it seems like a fish's view of the hull of an oared galley, frankly.) A dog and two men (one barely visible) in the right background are reacting to it, so it's not just a speck of water damage.

Obviously, flying saucers were part of any outdoor scene when this picture was made, and so the artist included one as part of the landscape, basically as filler.

Case closed. Flying saucers are real.

And if you've continued reading past the previous sentence, it's probably because you harbor a suspicion—perhaps even need to believe—that there are other explanations. You're in luck.

First, you might note that the picture—as defined by its title—concerns the birth of Jesus, and there he is, as an infant, on the right hand (your left) of the Virgin Mary. The other infant (standing) is Jesus' kinsman John the Baptist, who by Biblical authority is six months older. (In the New Testament they don't meet as children, but they do in some apocrypha, or church legends.)

And then you might note the contents of the New Testament, the Gospel According to Luke 2:8–20. This passage describes shepherds in the region of Bethlehem watching their flocks by night at the time of the nativity, and being confronted by an angel bearing news of the birth of Jesus. The angel's sight was glorious enough to fill them with fear, and before departing the angel was flanked with a "heavenly host" singing the praises of God and of peace on earth.

And so, on the Virgin's left (your right) you'll see in the distance two men on a hill with a dog and a barely visible flock—they're shepherds. The men and the dog are marveling at a thing in the sky from which radiates gold-flecked lines that presumably represent rays of light. It takes no great effort to believe that the artist is representing the heavenly host.

Meanwhile, in the sky on the Virgin's right (your left) is the Star of Bethlehem, which heralded the nativity in the New Testament. Below it are three smaller stars that have no biblical basis, but which stand for the three-fold purity of the Virgin Mary, before, during, and after the immaculate conception.

In the end, what you have is a fairly standard nativity scene, with Jesus on the Virgin's right and a landscape with at least one startled shepherd on her left.

The main difference is the additional presence, on her right, of the infant John the Baptist. Third parties were often added to nativity scenes if they were the patron of the church or town in question, so we can presume this picture was used in a church that designated John the Baptist as its patron saint.

What it obviously is not is a portrayal of a flying saucer. Every visual element of the painting was mandated by the church sponsor, whom the painter had to satisfy if he wanted to get paid. The visual elements themselves, meanwhile, were the products of centuries of Christian iconographic tradition, and the churchmen were no more likely to experiment with it than the painter was to experiment with the assigned subject matter. The personal artistic expression of the artist, or of the churchmen, was not an issue. There was too much money involved, and the religious subjects were too important. Maybe the artist would have felt more fulfilled doing something else, but that was irrelevant—this was a job. In fact, it's likely that artists of the time had nothing in their vocabulary to convey the concept of personal artistic expression. (Of course, they understood personal artistic satisfaction, as they had high technical standards.)

Basically, if the churchmen had wanted a picture of a flying saucer, they would have commissioned one, and the results would have been completely unambiguous. Over the centuries they found ways to deal with witches, plagues, barbarian invasions, earthquakes, feminism, protestants, Turks, and Galileo. Confronted with extraterrestrials, they would probably have formed a committee to deal with that challenge, too.

Finally, we might as well add that the attribution of the painting to Mainardi is tentative. Other sources name Jacopo del Sellaio (c. 1441–1493) or the obscure Maestro del Tondo Miller. All of them did similar Madonna pictures, with Jesus on the Virgin's right, with or without John the Baptist. Usually there's some livestock because the nativity took place in a barn, and there's some landscape in the background for the shepherds. It's as if they were working from the same script—which they were.

But Mainardi had them all beat: He had a brother-in-law named Domenico Ghirlandaio (1449–1494) who had a student named Michelangelo. Let's stick with him.

34
1710 Flying Saucers?

The 1710 Dutch painting "Baptism of Christ" appears to show a flying saucer, assuming it's not an image derived from the biblical account of the baptism of Christ. Baptism of Christ, c.1710 (oil on canvas) by Aert de Gelder (1645–1727) Fitzwilliam Museum, University of Cambridge, UK, through The Bridgeman Art Library. Used with permission.

The term *flying saucer* originated from a 1947 news report of what a businessman flying a private airplane near Mount Rainier complained of seeing in the sky. The concept is now synonymous with UFOs, especially the kind that is assumed to be carrying star-traveling benevolent extraterrestrials. (Why such craft should be shaped like saucers, as opposed to spheres, zeppelins, or Ferraris, remains obscure.)

So it's rather eye-catching that one shows up 237 years earlier in the 1710 48x37 cm oil painting "The Baptism of Christ" by Dutch painter and Rembrandt pupil Aert (or Arent) de Gelder (1645–1727) now hanging in the Fitzwilliam Museum in Cambridge, England. But there it is, a flat round object in the sky, beaming down light to illuminate the central figures (who would be, judging by the title, Jesus and John the Baptist).

We can interpret this two different ways:

- The artist is depicting an event that he actually witnessed, and has slipped it into a painting that is really supposed to be about something else. Obviously, flying saucers were common in the sky in 1710, and presumably earlier. The implication of their historical presence is that they are real objects in the sky, and not artifacts of subliminal suggestion introduced by a lifetime of exposure to modern pop culture and science fiction imagery. And if they are real objects that keep returning to our skies throughout the centuries, surely they are piloted by benevolent extraterrestrials.

- The "flying saucer" in this picture is a visual allegory in the tradition of Western religious artwork and iconography. Any resemblance to a UFO exists solely in the eye of a beholder whose expectations have been formed by a lifetime of exposure to the imagery of modern pop culture and science fiction.

To examine the first alternative, we need to look at Gelder himself and see if there is any likelihood that he was impacted by flying saucers. Gelder was a resident of Dordrecht, Holland, and is differentiated from his teacher Rembrandt mostly through his use of brighter colors. He was also a master of chiaroscuro, or the art of using light and dark contrasts. At first glance the technique mostly accentuates the absence of artificial lighting in Renaissance Holland. Typically, the faces of the subjects are delineated by the limited available light in whatever room or scene is being depicted, with everything else in the picture fading into an unlit background. But the technique also adds a three-dimensional quality to the work, with the lit objects pulling to the foreground.

Indeed, most of his work involves indoor settings lit with the kind of single-candle light source that Rembrandt made famous. Frankly, this does not leave much scope for depicting flying saucers. His other famous painting with an outdoor setting is "The Way to Golgotha," and it does show a considerable amount of sky, but there's nothing in it but overcast. So if he was eager to depict flying saucers, there is not much evidence of it.

But if flying saucers were hovering in the sky, surely Gelder was not the sole witness. The period in which he was active was not a contemplative age in which worldly affairs were discounted as irrelevant. Nor was it a pre-literate age in which few events got recorded. Actually, Holland and most of the countries of Europe had well-organized central governments that ran on paperwork. Holland and England especially supported large navies that pursued a series of naval wars with each other, and then allied with each other against Spain. For weather-assessment and navigation purposes navies paid a lot of attention to the sky, and the appearance there of flying saucers would have triggered governmental concern and comment (to say the least).

We have voluminous government archives from the era with no such reports. Of course, they could have been censored, but the archives of multiple governments would have had to have been censored, and some of those governments were mutually hostile.

Even if there was an entity powerful enough to cleanse multiple and mutually hostile government archives, there were private archives that would not have been detected at the time. For instance, we now have the encrypted shorthand diary of a British naval bureaucrat at the time (Samuel Pepys), which was not decrypted and published until more than a century after his death. Its details extend to explicit descriptions of extramarital sexual encounters. If things in the sky were a concern, Pepys would not have hesitated to mention it in his diary. He didn't—his chief concern remained the fear of his wife walking in on him with the servant girl.

So if there were widely witnessed UFO visitations, it stands to reason that a visual reference in one period painting would not have been the only evidence.

But the image is there. If it's not a picture of a flying saucer, what is it?

That brings us to the second interpretation, that it's a visual allegory within Christian iconographic traditions. Examining the flying saucer, we see that there's a tiny white speck in its center. Close examination shows that it is actually a white bird, like a dove.

And that brings us to the New Testament, the Gospel of John 1:32, describing the baptism of Jesus by John the Baptist, the latter having seen the Holy Spirit descend on Jesus "as a dove from heaven."

Meanwhile, the painting is titled "Baptism of Christ." Given the biblical description, depicting a dove within the scene would seem mandatory—and indeed you find one as soon as you look for it.

Why there's a bright round spot of light on the overcast sky above the dove is harder to explain. Certainly it's sharply delineated and is beaming light to the ground. But golden circles in the sky were used by other church painters to indicate the divine presence. Considering the way the light is illuminating the subjects, perhaps the painter was trying to depict a ray of light strong enough to pierce the overcast and reach the subjects, catching the dove in route.

On the other hand, paintings concerning John the Baptist were often commissioned as a gift to a specific church by a well-off parishioner who happened to be named John, or the local equivalent. There is usually some person in the crowd whose face is recognizably that of the donor, and the donor would have some say over the composition. There is no such person in Gelder's crowd, indicating that the depiction of the scene may have been entirely a matter of self-expression. If you wanted to say that Gelder was looking for a way to depict something in the sky and used this setting, you could say it. But you could also say that he was looking for a way to apply chiaroscuro in an outdoor setting.

Meanwhile, those surfing UFO-oriented Websites may come across versions of this image where the descending rays of light are more pronounced than they are in Gelder's original painting. In the original, the emphasis is on the middleground figures of Jesus and John the Baptist, framed by the other elements in the composition (including the light beams.) In the edited versions, the light beam acquires the main focus.

It appears that editing the classics is well within the power of a modern personal computer, something not foreseen by science fiction.

Be that as it may, when all is said and done the image is still there. You can look at it or look beyond it, and see what you choose to see. If you want to see the flying saucer, it will leap out at you. If you want to see the dove and the New Testament story, it will leap out at you. If the test of true art is that it is open to multiple interpretations, then this picture stands up to the test.

But it is probably not a good indication of what was happening the skies of Holland during Gelder's lifetime.

35

Independence Day, 1428?

This medieval painting appears to show flying saucers menacing Rome. Or the painting could be an attempt to illustrate a miracle that, legend has it, led to the building of a particular church in Rome in late antiquity. Public domain image from Wikimedia Commons.

Its release was timed for the lucrative July 4th holiday time-slot in 1996, and the Hollywood blockbuster *Independence Day* did not disappoint, going on to become the highest-grossing film of the year. The audience was treated to scenes of whole cities succumbing to attacks by non-benevolent extraterrestrials in huge flying saucers, intending to exploit the Earth's resources after first destroying the human race. The aliens hover over the doomed cities and generate super-hot ground-hugging clouds of fumes and dust (called pyroclastic flow) by pumping laser beams into the ground. For defense, the large flying saucers release clouds of small ones, also gray. Humanity is helpless until the heroes figure out how to launch a counterattack, which takes place on July 4, Independence Day in the United States.

A large gray saucer-like craft similarly appears to hover over Rome, attended by squadrons of smaller defensive saucers, in the 144x76 cm oil and tempera on wood painting "Miracle of the Snow," done in about 1428 by Masolino da Panicale (1383–c. 1447.) (The name means "Tommy from Panicale." His real name was Tommaso di Cristoforo Fini.) Now in the Museo di Capodimonte in Naples, Italy, it was originally part of an altar piece in the Church of Santa Maria Maggiore in what is now central Rome.

The official story behind this stiff, formal picture (also listed as the "Foundation of the Basilica of St. Mary the Greater") is that it depicts the legendary miracle that led to the founding of that particular church in late antiquity. (The church's name stems from the fact that it is the largest church devoted to Mary in Rome.) The legend is that several people (including the pope) had a simultaneous dream on the night of August 4–5, 358, involving a message from the Virgin Mary, that she would like a church built in Rome in her honor, and would mark the spot for the church with snowfall. One of the recipients of the dream was an elderly rich couple who were heirless, and had prayed to the Virgin Mary to reveal an heir to them. They were advised to use their money to build a church in honor of the Virgin.

Despite the summer heat, snow then fell on the top of Esquiline Hill on the morning of August 5. The snow on the ground formed the outline of a church, and persisted on the ground until the outline was staked out. (The Esquiline Hill was one of the original seven hills of Rome, and was a fashionable neighborhood to the northeast of the city center.)

Church histories frankly state that the legend did not surface until about a thousand years after the church was built, but that has not detracted from its subsequent annual celebration with a feast day on August 5. To commemorate the snow, white rose petals are dropped from the church dome.

In the picture, the snow has already fallen and the people on the ground are reacting to it. The picture shows Jesus and the Virgin Mary above the clouds, while below them the pope and other dignitaries trace the architectural outline made by the snow on the conveniently vacant plot of ground. The man in the foreground with a hoe is wearing a papal crown.

Midway between heaven and earth, the clouds are dark but are not otherwise reminiscent of snow clouds, being nearly lens-shaped, with well-defined borders. The bottoms are nearly flat, while the tops are somewhat fluffy. There is one main cloud, with about 30 smaller ones. Assuming they are all the same size, the smaller ones are presumably supposed to be farther away, trailing off into the distance. (However, it is not supposed to be snowing in the distance, only on the spot in the foreground.) Or, they could just be smaller clouds floating below the main one.

Basically, the clouds are not very realistic, but the people in the painting are stiff and formulaic, so we can assume the same approach was used with the clouds. Anyway, it is clear that the picture is not about the clouds, but about the people on the ground and in heaven. The clouds appear to be in the picture mainly to provide a division between heaven and earth. There are more than two dozen people on the ground, and only one (just to the right, in the background) is looking up at the clouds. (Due to repairs to the painting, two other people in the background appear to be headless.) Two others are talking to each other. As for the rest, their sole focus is the snow on the ground.

Meanwhile, the legend of "Our Lady of the Snows" exists independently from this painting, and has been depicted by other church artists, usually with more realistic heavy overcast rather than discrete UFO-like clouds.

Finally, Rome still exists, and so was apparently not turned into a smoking wasteland on the morning of August 5, 358, by hovering UFOs that pumped laser beams into the ground until pyroclastic flow covered the region. So the similarity between the 1428 and 1996 images can be dismissed as a coincidence.

All of which only proves (if anything) that the picture is what it purports to be: a depiction of the legend of the snow. But where did that legend come from? Could it commemorate some half-remembered UFO visit in the past?

Presumably, the legend of the snow itself does not, because it is based on miraculous snow in summer, with a miraculously precise accumulation. The nature or appearance of any associated snow clouds was not an issue. Actually, the falling of the snow being a miracle, no clouds were necessary. Had saucer-like star-faring craft appeared over Rome in late antiquity with hulls so cold that they triggered snow-like precipitation, you'd think the event would be reflected in more than one painting, especially a painting depicting a legend that itself did not circulate until a thousand years after the purported event.

Or could the image be based on something else Masolino saw in the sky at some point in his lifetime? If dismissing the UFO connection is not an option, then crediting the saucers to Masolino's visual memory seems more reasonable. He is known to have traveled as far afield as Hungary, and may have seen things in the sky that his fellow Italian artists missed. His other surviving works (at least those available on the Internet) depict indoor settings, so maybe the Santa Maria Maggiore altar piece was his sole opportunity to depict what he'd seen. It's only fair to say that no one can prove otherwise—or ever will, because you can't prove a negative.

But it's too bad he missed the movie—clearly, he would have loved the visual effects.

36
Laser in 1486?

This helpfully self-dated picture appears to show a flying saucer targeting a young women with a laser beam. Or, it could be illustrating a Bible story with some added municipal boosterism. Public domain image from Wikimedia Commons.

A flying saucer pokes down from a cloud and shoots a laser beam at the head of a woman through a tangle of Renaissance Italian architecture. If you're talking about the 207×147 cm oil painting "The Annunciation, with Saint Emidius," by Carlo Crivelli, hanging in the National Gallery in London, yes, the image is there.

At least at first glance it is. On closer inspection, there is so much going on in this painting—and the decision process behind some of it seems so questionable—that the inclusion of a random flying saucer doesn't seem all that odd. But, in the end, you have to question the presence of the flying saucer, too.

"The Annunciation" refers to the story in the New Testament of the announcement, by an angel (who's usually depicted as the Archangel Gabriel) to the Virgin Mary that she would miraculously give birth to a son, who could be called Jesus. The event is described in the Gospel of Mark 1:26–38. She took some convincing, so the scene offers dramatic potential for a portraitist. (If this does not sound familiar, you may be remembering the parallel account from the Gospel of Matthew in which her fiancée, Joseph, received a separate announcement during a dream—see Matthew 1:18–21.)

Because Jesus is assumed to have been born on Christmas Day in December, the Annunciation is assumed to have taken place nine months earlier, around the spring equinox, which typically falls on about March 25. The spring equinox was also the beginning of the year in some old-style calendars. The exact date of the commemoration is calculated by various methods, and the appointed day is called the Feast of the Annunciation.

It so happens that on the Feast of the Annunciation in 1486 the town of Ascoli Piceno in the Papal States in east-central Italy was granted partial self-rule by Pope Sixtus IV, otherwise famous as the builder of the Sistine Chapel. (A later pope, Julius II, decided that the ceiling was boring and commissioned Michelangelo to paint it.) Thereafter, the Feast of the Annunciation would also be commemorated as the town's independence day.

Residing in Ascoli Piceno was portraitist Carlo Crivelli (c. 1430–c. 1494). He was a native of the port city of Venice who left Venetian territory and moved inland to landlocked Ascoli Piceno after spending six months in jail in about 1457 for adultery involving the wife of a sailor. Freed from maritime distractions, he became successful painting altar pieces, and was commissioned to do one for the dual commemorations of Ascoli Piceno's 1486 Feast of the Annunciation.

The result is a highly complex piece of work into which is crammed a wide range of images, executed with a high standard of technical precision. There are two motifs, religious and municipal. (Okay, there are three if you count the UFO.)

The religious motif includes the Virgin Mary, at the lower right, circumspectly reading in private, in a devotional posture at a kneeling bench. She is studying a book, which we can assume is the Old Testament, because she is often depicted reading prophecy concerning herself in the Book of Isaiah 7:14. The textiles on the shelf may refer to the non-biblical legend that she was raised in the Temple of Jerusalem where she wove priestly garments.

A dove rides a beam of light down to her head, somehow missing her halo. A dove combined with the beam of light traditionally represents her immaculate conception through the intervention of the Holy Spirit, one of the three persons of God in the Christian Trinity. For obscure reasons (or just because it looked better) the beam is always shown descending at an angle rather than straight down. The room she is in is as well-lit as the outside, illuminated by the light of faith and signifying the banishment of the forces of darkness.

She is stationed in front of a barred window looking onto the street. In the street is the Archangel Gabriel, with the traditional wings and a halo. He seems to be looking at her, but is not saying anything, and appears to be out of speaking range anyway. He is holding a white flower, to signify purity and indicate that all this is happening in the spring. (The cucumber and apple on the ground doubtless had some meaning, now obscure.)

Then we get to the municipal motif: leaning over the angel's shoulder as if trying to get his attention is St. Emidius. The traditional way of showing that a saint was the patron of a place was to show him or her holding a scale model of the place, and St. Emidius is indeed shown holding a model of downtown Ascoli Piceno. In fact, he's holding it as if hoping the angel will approve it. The angel is not really paying much attention to him, though, and is merely holding up his hand in blessing, either of the town or the Virgin, or both. (Or, he's distractedly motioning St. Emidius to get out of the way during this important moment. After all, true art is supposed to be open to multiple interpretations.)

The municipal motif continues in the faux inscription along the bottom: LIBERTAS ECCLESIASTICA (Freedom of the Church) along with the coat of arms of the pope and the local bishop. Above it, on the bottom of the left-hand house pillar, is Crivelli's credit line, with the date on the right-hand pillar.

St. Emidius is also called St. Emygdius, reflecting the fact that he was a native of Germany. He was a Christian martyr who had a career as a healer and bishop. He was decapitated in Ascoli Piceno in about 309 by the Pagan Roman governor for refusing to participate in official worship. He then picked up his own head, walked up a nearby mountain, and constructed a still-extant chapel. (He appears uninjured in the painting, but that may reflect his career as a healer.) Tradition has it that his local protection has been successfully invoked against depredations of Visgoths in 409, against a plague in 1038, against earthquakes several times since 1703, and against the depredations of German troops in 1943. His personal feast day is August 5.

So obviously, the painting is a mishmash of unrelated, even clashing iconography. St. Emidius lived three centuries after the Annunciation, which took place in the Holy Land, a long way from the Italian town of Ascoli Piceno, and 1,486 years before 1486. The New Testament records no visit to Ascoli Piceno by the Virgin Mary or the Archangel Gabriel (or by anyone else). In fact, it does not mention Ascoli Piceno in any context. Nor does it mention the presence of St. Emidius (or any other third party) at the Annunciation.

Just as obviously, the devout Catholic churchmen and municipal boosters who commissioned the painting knew all that and didn't care—they wanted a painting that somehow celebrated their local dual-purpose commemoration of the Feast of the Annunciation, and Crivelli delivered. Hopefully, anyone suggesting a similar project in this day and age would be shouted down on grounds of cheap blasphemy. But in 1486 people were burned at the stake for asking too many questions.

With these wild juxtapositions going on, the third motif doesn't seem all that out of place. Yes, there's also a flying saucer in the upper left, beaming a laser at the Virgin through a strategically placed wall vent.

But, alas, closer inspection brings us back to two motifs, as analysis of the third (UFO) motif shows that it is not really there. It's based on an apparent laser beam shooting down from a flying saucer floating in the somewhat cloudy sky in the upper left. But as mentioned earlier, the laser beam is actually part of the traditional depiction of the intervention of the Holy Spirit—the dove gives it away. Admittedly, the strategic placing of the wall vent so that the beam could reach the Virgin is just too gratuitous, and it seems amazing that Crevelli's patrons let him get away with it. Evidently, it was assumed that she had to be kept safely inside, but the archangel and the overshadowing Holy Spirit had to be outside where St. Emidius could get their attention.

That leaves us with the so-called flying saucer. In low-resolution images it does look like a glowing round object in the clouds. But higher resolution shows it is a glowing cloud with two concentric circles of angels. The faces and halos of some are clearly visible.

In other words, it's a vortex of angels, a device often used in church art to represent the presence of the Supreme Being. The image is not exactly biblical, but does show up in Dante's "Paradise" (Canto 31).

So we're left with religious imagery. Crivelli was giving the customers what they wanted, not showing us what was happening in the sky in 1486. But if there ever was a painting that will lead you in to trouble if you take it literally, it's this one.

37
UFOs in 1350?

The presence of the flying objects in the top right and left corners
of this 1350 fresco in a dome in a monastery in Kosovo could
indicate that the artists had seen UFOs. Or they could indicate
that the artists were adhering to long-standing iconographic
traditions. The vertical chains support light fixtures.
BLAGO Fund Inc. USA.

There they are on either side of Christ on the cross. They look like they are supposed to represent little manned spacecraft shooting through the air at the edges of the scene. Some call them UFOs, but you could also say that they look like Mercury capsules from the early days of the American space program, with a round heat shield at one end. (Admittedly, the "astronauts" are facing the wrong direction, and the Mercury capsules had squared rather than pointed sterns.) In fact, the images were "discovered" about 1963, when Project Mercury was getting a lot of press coverage.

The problem is that they were painted more than 600 years earlier, between about 1335 and 1350. Do they record a medieval UFO visit? Or do they reflect some foreknowledge of Project Mercury?

Or, are they another example of the old joke about "locomotive lung," a medical condition so-named because it made the victim's breathing sound like the wheezing of a steam locomotive? Oddly enough, the condition was unheard of before about 1830, when steam locomotives came along, or after about 1950, when diesel locomotives took over. Surely there must be a reason....

The images are part of the frescoes that cover about every available wall space in the Orthodox Serbian monastery of Visoki Decani, just south of the city of Pec, in a river valley amidst the mountains of western Kosovo, not far from the Albanian border. It's touted as being the best preserved medieval monastery in Kosovo. Aside from that, the monastery is famous as the burial place of Serbian King Stefan Uros III Decanski—and for having those UFOs in the Crucifixion scene, located inside the wall of the dome, third level, part 2.

One of the UFOs is in the upper right-hand corner of the scene, is predominantly silver, and contains a long-haired and presumably female figure looking backward over her shoulder toward the cross, giving the impression that the craft is moving away from the cross.

The other is in the upper left-hand corner of the screen and is predominamtly red. It contains a short-haired presumably male figure in a cloak looking straight ahead toward the cross, giving the impression that it is moving towards the cross.

And this is where the UFO believers and the art historians part company. To UFO believers, the objects are depictions of the unidentified flying objects that populate the sky, today as in 1350. Obviously, they were innocently included by the medieval Serbian artists, who were just depicting in the sky the things they normally see in the sky, unaware that such things would later be suppressed.

To art historians, they are part of a rich iconographic tradition of Byzantine and medieval church art involving depictions of the crucifixion. They represent the sun (red) and the moon (silver.) The sun is typically (but not always) on Christ's right (your left) hand, with the moon on the other side. If there is a gender portrayal, the sun is male and the moon is female. Usually, though, they look more like orbs with faces than Mercury capsules.

The inclusion of the sun and moon are presumed to be reminders of the Gospels of Matthew, Mark, and Luke, which state that, during the crucifixion, darkness fell between noon and 3 p.m. Possibly this is why the sun and moon are depicted as moving, to indicate that the light is changing. They could also be seen as representing the Old and New Testaments, indicating that the former (which is outbound) could now only be understood through the light shone by the latter (which is inbound.) Additionally, the use of a sun icon to show that heaven has taken an interest in the person or event in question goes back at least to Roman times.

The meanings of the other aspects of the iconography—red male right-hand for the sun, female silver left-hand for the moon—remain obscure but doubtless have ancient origins. But their use indicates that the churchman who commissioned the frescoes had precise specifications, founded on well-established graphic traditions, and that nothing appears in the images by accident. The artists were standing on scaffolds in the rotunda of a new edifice funded by the king, and they were not there for purposes of self-expression. They were there to satisfy a paying customer, and slipping in a couple of UFOs in the corners of one picture just to let future generations know they'd seen them was not going to happen.

But, of course, maybe these things were so commonly seen in the skies that they would be included in any outdoor scene as a matter of course. Alas, they only show up in the Crucifixion panel, and only in ways that satisfy iconographic traditions.

And if they are meant to represent real objects, you have to admit that they don't look very real. If they are spacecraft, they are spacecraft that are completely transparent, contain only one passenger each, and have barely enough room for that passenger. Meanwhile, the passengers are dressed in street clothes. (In fact, the presumably female figure is apparently topless, but has demurely turned away from the audience.) If real spacecraft were in the habit of landing in medieval Kosovo, surely the astronauts would be dressed quite differently.

So even a UFO true believer would probably concede that the objects are not supposed to be taken as photorealistic images of things seen in the sky. If they are not allegorical images from the Byzantine tradition, perhaps they are crude schematics, showing that a person was inside a cone-shaped object in the sky.

So we are back to Project Mercury, whose spacecraft had about the same proportions (in terms of passenger to spacecraft dimensions) as the objects in the fresco. But that also brings us back to locomotive lung. The Mercury capsules were glorified escape pods incapable of any space travel beyond low orbit and re-entry—forget star travel. But in 1963 they were a visual metaphor for space travel. Likewise, for 120 years, the wheezing of a steam engine was a metaphor for a certain lung condition. In both cases we have moved on, and today we have to convince ourselves that the objects in the frescoes are supposed to be spacecraft.

Basically, we don't know what the hardware required for interstellar travel will look like—but chances are it won't look like anything currently in use. When we do perfect the technology we can look back and see if any early painters might actually have seen something like it. When that day comes maybe someone will owe someone else an apology.

But until then we have to rely on logic.

ASTRONOMICAL CANDIDATES

It's monumental hubris to say that an astronomical body is out of place, either in time or space. After all, there it is. The laws of physics that govern its motions and other behaviors are known with precision. Space probes can be made to rendezvous with it. As for how it got there, detailed scientific theories explain the whole process back to the Big Bang, and possibly beyond. For generations people have been complaining (or gloating) that science has removed the necessity of God, except perhaps as the Cosmic Billiards Player who put the balls in motion. Etc.

Excuse me—the real hubris is in accepting the previous paragraph without blinking. For millennia we have gazed at the stars with nearly total incomprehension, and things are only superficially better today. Meanwhile, what facts we have been able to piece together concerning the nature of the cosmos are totally at odds with our daily experience. But not only are we able to live in comfortable denial about them, we may also be better off doing so.

Trivial example: If you got up early enough this morning you were able to see the sun rise gloriously in the east, its rosy fingers touching the clouds across a background that was fading from dark to pale blue. Alas, in truth the sun didn't rise—the Earth on which you were standing rotated in such a way that the sun came into view. You (hopefully) knew that, but the illusion of the sun rising is too persistent to disregard. Nor is there any reason to disregard it. No one gets confused, or accuses you of trying to mislead them, if you refer to the sun rising. In fact, if you insisted on referring to the Earth as rotating under us, or corrected other people who referred to the sun rising, you might not get an entirely favorable response.

In other words, it is accepted without discussion that we are better off ignoring selected information about this prosaic topic. Describing it in full involves too much information, and some of it is disquieting. If we thought them at length, our equilibrium might suffer. For most of us, celestial mechanics is out of place.

As it turns out, our relationship with a couple of places in the Solar System has been entirely based on decisions to ignore disquieting information.

They're undeniably out there, but our equilibrium would suffer if we thought about them at length. In terms of a cosmos that satisfies our need for pat explanations, they are out of place.

The first is Iapetus, the major moon of Saturn that is farthest from the planet and has the most tilted orbit. When astronomers first discovered it three centuries ago it seemed to be playing peek-a-boo with them. They decided to ignore this fact, assuming a rational theory would eventually explain the behavior. The theory has since been confirmed—and supplemented with reams of new, stunningly inexplicable information, hinting that something really weird happened out there. Meanwhile, Iapetus managed to enter the public consciousness pretty much on its own. Millions of people who have never heard of it (or could name any moon of any other outer planet) have been awed by a story inspired by the existence of Iapetus.

The other place is Martian orbit, where you'll find the two moons of Mars. They managed to enter the public consciousness a century and a half before they were discovered. Yes, before they were discovered. But that level of weirdness is only appropriate considering the scale of the disquiet, and the damage to our equilibrium that the information about them poses. Finding a comfortable level of denial about the information is doubtless our best bet, until such time as we come to terms with it.

Until then, when next the sun escapes from its nightly imprisonment in the underworld and returns in glory to the eastern horizon, do greet it with appropriate appreciation.

38
Saturn's Mystery Moon

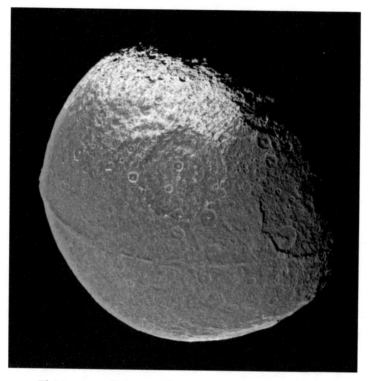

Three-quarter-lit Iapetus showing the mysterious dark spot that covers nearly an entire hemisphere, and the equally mysterious equatorial ridge that extends in a straight line across the dark spot.
NASA/JPL/Space Science Institute.

Perhaps awesome mysteries await anyone who examines any natural phenomenon in sufficient detail. But you don't have to delve very deeply to have that experience when talking about Iapetus (eye-Ap-a-Tus), the outmost of the large, prograde moons of Saturn. It is 914 miles in diameter and orbits Saturn at a distance of 2.2 million miles. The fact that it is large enough to be spherical and has a prograde orbit (that is, its orbital travel is in the same direction as Saturn's day-night spin) indicates that it was formed with that planet—it's a "regular" moon of Saturn. (The next section examines the significance of "prograde" and "regular" moon.) Iapetus differs from Saturn's other regular moons by its rather large orbital inclination, of more than 15 degrees. And while that inclination is a mystery, that's not the mystery (actually, mysteries) we're talking about.

The first mystery involving Iapetus is that, when it was first discovered, it was observed to disappear and reappear. Large astronomical bodies are, of course, not supposed to do that.

The moon was first observed in 1671 by pioneering Italian-French astronomer Giovanni Cassini. After figuring its orbit and following it for a number of months, he realized that he could see Iapetus when it was on one side of Saturn, but not when it was on the other side. It was a time when irrational factors were still given credence in the public mind—the Salem witch trials were 20 years in the future, to give one small example. But Cassini was a man of science and would have none of it. He immediately assumed that Iapetus had a bright highly reflective side and a dark, non-reflective side. Meanwhile, he assumed that it revolved only once during its orbit around Saturn, meaning that one side always faced Saturn. Therefore, he could see Iapetus only when it was positioned so that its bright side faced Earth, which was during half its orbit around Saturn. During the rest of its orbit its dark side faced the Earth and Iapetus could not be picked out of the dark background of space.

He could point to the example of the Earth's moon, which is locked in position so that one side always faces the Earth. And he knew that the power of available telescopes was a moving target, and what could not be seen today might be seen with a better telescope tomorrow. But that did not mean that the thing that could not be seen did not exist in the meantime.

Basically, better telescopes let you see dimmer objects—ones with lower "apparent magnitude." The apparent magnitude refers to the brightness of an object when seen by an observer on Earth, and takes no account of how brilliant the object would be if you were nearby—that would be its "absolute magnitude." Extremely bright stars that are far away will have low apparent magnitudes, even though they may have high absolute magnitudes.

However, in the magnitude scale used by astronomers (both apparent and absolute), dimmer objects are assigned higher numbers. Apparent magnitude 1 is a bright star, while magnitude 6 is about the faintest star that can be seen with the unaided eye on a dark, clear night. (In the night sky of a city, you might not be able to see anything dimmer than 3, as dimmer stars than that are washed out by the background glow.) Values higher than 6 will require a telescope, and the higher the value the fancier the telescope will have to be. On the other end of the scale, objects brighter than 0 are given negative values.

For example, the Pole Star (Polaris) is about 2, Sirius is -1.4, Venus at its brightest is almost -5, and Jupiter and Mars at their brightest are almost -3. The full moon is almost -13.

When Cassini found Iapetus, it had an apparent magnitude of 10—when he could see it. He kept the faith for more than 30 years, assuming he could eventually find it when he had equipment that was good enough. That finally happened in 1705, and he found that its dim side had an apparently magnitude of 12. Because each full level of magnitude is about 2.5 times brighter (or dimmer) than the next, the bright side of Iapetus turned out to be more than six times brighter than the dark side. That's an average based on whole hemispheres. Modern measurements show that its dark areas are as dark as fresh asphalt, while the bright areas are as bright as arctic ice, or 10 times more reflective.

So Cassini had demonstrated a rational explanation—except that it was not really an explanation, because there was no obvious mechanism for producing the bright-dark difference. Also, why isn't the division observed with any other moons?

True, it might result from some kind of sand-blasting effect because, with one side always facing Saturn, another side a quarter-turn away would always be facing the direction of orbit. Saturn has obvious rings, so maybe there is a lot of debris even out in the vicinity of Iapetus, which orbits 1.9 million miles beyond the rings.

Meanwhile, the idea of this moon amounting to an unexplained blinking light in the Solar System intrigued more than one writer, which brings us to Iapetus' impact on popular culture: Iapetus was the objective of the space mission described in the 1968 Arthur C. Clarke novel, *2001: A Space Odyssey.* (The novel was adapted from a 1951 short story by Clarke titled "Sentinel to Eternity.") Explorers on Earth's moon find a buried monolith that is obviously artificial, and when sunlight first falls on it after excavation it beams a radio message to Iapetus. When an astronaut gets to Iapetus to investigate (surviving an onboard computer's murder of the rest of the crew) he finds a "gate" that allows interstellar travel.

In the enigmatic movie adaptation, the moon is switched to Jupiter, because a visually convincing movie version of Saturn's rings proved too difficult.

A real, albeit unmanned spaceship did reach Iapetus in 2007, six years later than Clark's projected date and 10 years after the probe—called *Cassini*—was launched jointly by NASA, the European Space Agency, and the Italian Space Agency. Having achieved orbit of Saturn in 2004, it performed a close pass of Iapetus in 2007.

As predicted, its pictures showed that a large part of one hemisphere was covered with a dark spot, not unlike a thin layer of soot. They named the dark spot Cassini Regio. The rest of the surface appears to be ice, and the border with Cassini Regio is abrupt, with no intermediate gray areas. If the dark spot was caused by scouring space debris, you'd expect Iapetus to wobble somewhat in its orbit, and so the darkness would have a feathered edge. The abrupt border makes it seem that the dark material was deposited in one incident, such as an explosion.

Within Cassini Regio, exactly following the moon's equator, is a pockmarked ridge of mountains, running straight as a garden wall, that's 12 miles wide and 8 miles high. It's so obvious in the space probe photos that commentators said it makes the moon look like a walnut. The ridge does not extend beyond the dark spot. (Before someone runs off and says the range is a military fortification that was defeated by the explosion that caused the dark spot, let's say that the mountains don't look artificial. They do look like a mountain range, with foothills, rather than a wall.)

Meanwhile, the moon's shape is oblate, the poles being somewhat flattened. The degree of flatness there, considering that the moon is almost entirely ice, would indicate that Iapetus spins every 10 hours. But it doesn't—it spins at the same rate that it orbits Saturn, or once every 79 days.

Basically, it looks like Cassini Regio was seared by a huge explosion (military or otherwise), but that does not explain the oddly limited equatorial mountain range, of the polar flattening. The best that can be said is that Iapetus has had an eventful history, one we may wish to understand, as we live in the same Solar System.

Like Giovanni Cassini, we should assume there's a rational explanation, even as Iapetus continues to produce phenomena that confounds us. But we may also have to accept the possibility that we may not understand Iapetus for the foreseeable future—it may be the ultimate reverse anachronism from the future.

But at least Iapetus was introduced into popular culture after it was discovered, rather than before. You'd think that would be a fundamental expectation—except that it doesn't apply to our next two subjects.

39
Those Inconvenient Martian Moons

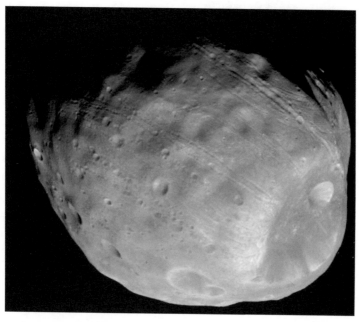

Phobos, one of the two moons of Mars, which were described a century and a half before they were discovered. Image courtesy NASA/ JPL-Caltech/University of Arizona.

Deimos and Phobos are the only moons of Mars. As moons go, they're tiny and irregular, being about the size of Mount Everest, or about 6 by 10 miles in the case of Deimos (the smaller, outermost moon), and 18 by 11 miles in the case of Phobos. Far too faint for the naked eye, and lost in the glare of Mars, seeing them requires a top-shelf astronomical telescope.

They were described in some detail in Jonathan Swift's *Gulliver's Travels* written in 1725. They were also mentioned in a short story by Voltaire in 1750.

Inconveniently for the facts mentioned in the previous paragraph, the moons were not discovered until 1877.

Doubtless you're waiting for a rational explanation. And you're not alone. But there might actually be one—although it requires that we assume that we are dealing with a mind-boggling, genuine coincidence. The result might not be as satisfying as an irrational explanation, but there are actual clues that support it. To find those clues, let's start examining the two pre-discovery descriptions of the moons. (If you'd prefer irrational explanations, don't stop here—read on to the end.)

The description from 1750 appears to be derivative and doesn't require much attention. It involves a short story by French Enlightenment philosopher Voltaire, titled "Micromegas," about a space alien from Sirius who is 20,000 feet tall, with a sidekick from Saturn who is somewhat smaller. Upon visiting Earth, the title character is startled to find that certain of the planet's tiny inhabitants somehow assume that the universe was created for their express benefit.

En route the two extraterrestrials happened to pass Mars. The narrator mentions that it has two moons that have so far escaped the attention of Earth's astronomers, and some argue against their existence. There is no further description of the moons (although the aliens disdain Mars as too small to land on). Because by 1750 there had been no scientific description of any such moons, we can presume that Voltaire is referring to a description of the moons in an extremely popular novel that had been out for a couple of decades, Swift's *Gulliver's Travels*.

Turning to that earlier description, things get really interesting. *Gulliver's Travels*, of course, is a satire on human behavior, politics, and travel books, and has been in print since it was written by Irish writer and clergyman Jonathan Swift in 1726. The reference to Mars and its moons occurs in the chapter about the fictional land of Balnibarbi, which is ruled by a king who lives on the floating island of Laputa. (In answer to the question silently forming in the minds of those readers who know Spanish, Swift presumably did know that "la puta" means "the whore.") The king enforces his will against malcontents by threatening to put them in the shade of his island, drop rocks on them, or simply land on them and crush them. He and his courtiers on the flying island, who have no contact with the ground, excel in music and mathematics but can barely even hold a conversation about any other subject, or even manage to make functional clothes or houses. They largely ignore their women, who are not allowed to leave the flying island because they never seem to want to return.

The information about Mars is presented as an example of the kind of advanced discoveries that the astronomers on Laputa had achieved compared to their European counterparts, despite or because of their lack of social and practical skills. This includes cataloging three times more fixed stars, tracking 93 different comets, and discovering those moons of Mars.

Simply mentioning the discovery of the moons would have been sufficient for Swift's purpose, which was to bolster his point about the danger of valuing science above culture, the danger of having a ruling class that is out of touch with the populace, and the tediousness of geeks. But he then goes on to describe the orbital characteristics of those moons.

Swift specifies that the inner one orbits Mars at a distance of three planetary diameters and has an orbital period of 10 hours. The outer one has an orbital distance of five diameters and a period of 21.5 hours.

And that's where things get eerie, because in 1877 the American astronomer Asaph Hall discovered Phobos and Deimos. Phobos orbits Mars at a distance of 1.4 planetary diameters and has an orbital period of 7.6 hours. Deimos orbits Mars at a distance of 3.5 planetary diameters and has an orbital period of 30.3 hours.

To recap:

Innermost v. Phobos / 3 v. 1.4 diameters / 10 v. 7.6 hours.

Outermost v. Deimos / 5 v. 3.5 diameters / 21.5 v. 30.3 hours.

If Swift was going to be this accurate and hint at genuine foreknowledge, why didn't he go on and be completely accurate? The simplest answer is that he had no foreknowledge. Assuming there's a rational answer, the clues indicate that he invented the moons to make a point, and got lucky.

The clues lie in the rest of the paragraph in the original book, which mention that the orbital characteristics of the moons are such that the square of their orbital periods are in proportion to the cube of their orbital distances, showing that they are governed by the same law of gravity that governs other celestial bodies.

Without naming it, Swift was referring to Kepler's Third Law of Planetary Motion, published about a century earlier by pioneering astronomer and mathematician Johannes Kepler. If D is the orbital diameter and P is the orbital period, $D^3 = P^2$. Notice that this law was based on proportions rather than actual values of speed and distance—that would not be possible until Newton published his laws of gravity, and astronomers refined their distance measurements after about 1670.

Before Swift wrote the novel, astronomers had confirmed that Kepler's Third Law applied to the orbits of the planets, and to the moons of Jupiter and Saturn. By showing it applied to a newly discovered system of planetary satellites, the Laputa astronomers backed the theory that the law described a universal force. Swift was promoting the idea that gravity was a universal force, affecting astronomical bodies exactly as it did objects on Earth, and that special rules did not govern the celestial realm.

But to demonstrate the applicability of the law, the invented satellite system had to have two moons, otherwise no proportion could be established. This is the case with the Earth and its moon.

So, Swift assigned Mars two moons, and gave them orbital values that made the Keplerian math easier. Remember, the law is based on proportions, not actual values. Accordingly we'll set the values of Swift's innermost moon to 1. As for the outmost moon, its orbital diameter is 1.66 times that of the innermost moon, and its orbital period is 2.15 times that of the innermost moon. According to the law, 1.66 cubed ought to be equal to 2.15 squared. And they more or less are—both are approximately equal to 4.6.

Swift's system of Martian moons does support Kepler's laws. But that is no mystery, assuming that Swift invented them for that purpose. Presumably he did the math, like any diligent author of a reliable travel book.

It's still eerie that his invented satellite system so closely matched the moons that were discovered a century and a half later. The situation almost begs for genuine foreknowledge on the part of Swift.

But if he did have foreknowledge, the orbital characteristics of his invented moons ought to fit the proportions established by Phobos and Deimos. The short answer is that Phobos and Deimos do exhibit orbital characteristics that fit Kepler's Third Law. That's no surprise as they are real celestial bodies governed by the laws of gravity whose interactions are described by Kepler's laws. But what happens if we add Swift's moons to the Phobos/Deimos system? Sparing the reader the math, is answer is that it doesn't work—when using ratios such that Phobos' orbital diameter and period equal 1, the Keplerian proportions for Swift's moons are off by a factor of almost six.

The implications are that Swift's moons would not have behaved as described in the real Martian gravity system, and therefore must have been invented without any real knowledge of Phobos and Deimos. Nor was the description of their orbital characteristics based on any real knowledge of gravity.

In other words, he guessed. Earth had one moon and Jupiter at the time was known to have four, so maybe he figured that two would be a good number for Mars, because it's between the Earth and Jupiter. He needed at least two to demonstrate Kepler's Law, and three would have meant added work.

He happened to guess right. That fact that the invented orbits vaguely resembled those of the real moons is a fluke. There's no mystery, and no real reverse anachronism.

But it's eerie nonetheless. And, you have to wonder why Swift felt compelled to invent moons around Mars, of all places. If he wanted to show off the skill of his fictional astronomers he had the entire cosmos to work with. Is there something so unconsciously important about the idea of Martian moons that he felt compelled to invent them and then write about them?

So here we get to the previously promised alternate, irrational explanation (which can, incidentally, coexist with the rational one). Perhaps the Martian moons represent something that has had (or will have) a major impact on the collective psyche of humanity, so that we feel unconsciously compelled to pay attention to them. (After all, as far as astronomical objects go, they're trivial.) Perhaps they're involved in mankind's distant past. Or, given prevalence of reverse anachronisms of the second kind (i.e., from the future) that keep showing up in this book, perhaps they're involved in an important event in humanity's future.

Or perhaps both—read the next section.

40

It Gets Better

The so-called Phobos monolith resembles a silo sticking out of the ground. If that's what it is, it would say something profound about the history of the Solar System, and explain some odd facts about the moons of Mars. Or it could just be an oddly symmetrical boulder. US Geological Survey.

If the literary situation with Martian moons Deimos and Phobos is eerie, then the basic astronomical facts about them may rise to the level of alarming. They present two basic problems:

1. They should not be there.
2. Something has been spotted on Phobos that looks like it should not be there.

As for their being there, the problem is that they are, for all intents, physically identical to many of the objects found in the asteroid belt between Mars and Jupiter. So it's natural to assume that Mars captured a few strays. The question is, how? Basically, some planets are equipped to capture moons, and some are not. Mars is not.

The ones clearly equipped to do it are the outer planets: Jupiter, Saturn, Uranus, and Neptune. All have retrograde moons, which proves that they are in the moon-capturing business, because retrograde moons have to have been captured.

Let's explain: The planets in question are all gas giants with a retinue of moons that are in prograde orbits, meaning they orbit around their planet in the same direction that the planet rotates in its day-night spin. Presumably, the disk of primal material that gave rise to the planet was rotating in that direction, and the moons congealed from the outer rim of that disk at the same time that the planet was congealing at the center. The orbits of such moons typically have low eccentricities (meaning they are closer to circles than ovals) and low inclinations (meaning their orbital planes are close to the planet's equator).

Additionally, they all have some retrograde moons, meaning that those moons orbit in the opposite direction that the planet is spinning and therefore could not have formed with the planet. Most are asteroid-sized, like Phobos and Deimos. They are assumed to have been captured from solar orbit.

So far, so good—but to be captured by a planet, an object has to, basically, fall toward the planet and sling-shot around it rather than hit it, and then fail to escape from it. But the velocity that any object picks up while falling toward a planet ought to be enough to let it continue on and escape from the planet after being sling-shot around it. There must be some force to slow it down so that it does not escape back into space.

The gas giants have two features that could (and apparently do) provide this force: thick atmospheres, and their retinue of moons. An incoming asteroid could graze the top of the atmosphere enough to be slowed down, but not crash into the planet. Alternately (or additionally) it could happen to swing past one of the planet's moons, whose gravity would provide some braking. (The newcomer could end up in a prograde orbit, incidentally, but would probably have an orbit with high eccentricity and inclination.)

However, this mechanism does not seem to work with the inner, or terrestrial planets (Mercury, Venus, Earth, and Mars.) The primal disks from which they congealed produced rocky balls rather than gas giants, with no retinue of prograde moons. (The Earth has one prograde moon that appears to have been produced by a now-defunct Mars-sized planet hitting the Earth at a 45-degree angle in the early days of the Solar System.) Additionally, the thick atmosphere that the gas giants use to provide braking is not there.

So, basically, Mars is not equipped to capture Deimos and Phobos. Did they capture themselves? It's a chicken-or-egg situation.

Meanwhile, their orbital characteristics do not indicate that they were ever captured. Their eccentricity is very low, and the orbit of Deimos is nearly a perfect circle. But something that was captured after failing to sling-shot around the planet ought to be in an obviously oval orbit. Meanwhile, the planes of the orbits of Deimos and Phobos are within a degree of the plane of Mars' equator. But the Martian equator is tilted about 25 degrees away from the Solar System's average orbital plane (the ecliptic). You'd think any incoming asteroids would retain their original orbital plane, and not end up with one that matches that of the Martian equator.

Maybe they, like Earth's moon, were also formed from impact debris. But that brings us back to those orbital characteristics. If Deimos and Phobos are congealed debris, that means their raw material was blasted fairly randomly into space. How did they both end up in circular orbits that parallel the Martian equator? The Earth's moon, which apparently did congeal from debris that was blasted into space, has an orbit around the Earth that is tilted about 5 degrees from the ecliptic.

And so Deimos and Phobos are out of place in an otherwise tightly policed Solar System. There are two schools of thought about this:

1. Their capture was the result of some freakish event. Perhaps they were orbiting each other (as certain asteroids have been seen to do) when they were captured. Some kind of gravitational harmonics could have produced the tidy orbits. Something must have—after all, there they are.

2. They're artificial satellites.

The first option is not a complete wimp-out. Neptune, for instance, has a fairly large moon named Triton with a vanishing small orbital eccentricity but whose retrograde orbit shows it was captured. But its orbit has substantial inclination and its capture can be explained through the usual gas giant procedures.

As for that second option, you'd expect the moons to be made of sheet metal. Modern space probe photos show that they look like charcoal briquettes that someone used for target practice with a BB gun—as is the case with most asteroids. But if they are millions of years old, the "charcoal" could be accumulated space debris encrusting the original structure. In that case you'd expect density calculations to show that they are hollow.

And such calculations show that Phobos, at least, is about 30-percent hollow. Meanwhile, Fobos 2, one of the last Soviet space probes, made a landing attempt in 1989 and, shortly before it stopped responding, managed to report that Phobos was leaking water vapor.

Of course, Phobos and Deimos could just be made of low-density, loosely packed material, with some ice content, as may be the case with many small, naturally occurring asteroids or comet fragments. But they could still have been placed in their orbits around Mars by artificial means. Their neat orbits would have facilitated rendezvous and docking by spacecraft, making them great waystations for Solar System navigation, both inbound to Mars and outbound from Mars. Components for rocket fuel could also have been mined from their minerals and ice, making space travel enormously easier. (Having to lift fuel from the surface is a huge impediment to space navigation. But if fuel is waiting for you when you get into orbit, everything changes.) Those same minerals and water could have been used to make the rocket fuel needed to maneuver each asteroid into its orbit, although it may have taken decades.

Again, if Deimos and Phobos were used for that purpose millions of years ago, there might not be any visible evidence remaining, thanks to the subsequent barrage of space debris. Not much, anyway. And that's where we get to that thing on Phobos that looks like it shouldn't be there.

The so-called Phobos monolith was found in a 1998 photo by NASA's Mars Global Surveyor probe. Its shadow makes it resemble a silo sticking out of the ground. Little else can be said about it due to the available resolution. It may just be an oddly symmetrical boulder that was given a long shadow by the low sun angle. Photos of the adjacent surface occasionally show obvious rocks with shadows, but those objects are much smaller. Meanwhile, the ground around the monolith shows the usual eroded craters, but also some blisters or raised spots, as if there were other objects just under the surface.

(Note that the Phobos monolith is not to be confused with the so-called Face on Mars formation that showed up in a 1976 *Viking I* orbital photo. As the name implies, it's on the surface of Mars, not on Phobos, although the tabloids have happily moved it to other planets as well. Photos of the feature by later Mars probes at higher resolutions are far more suggestive of an eroded plateau than a face.)

Of course, the monolith may just be a smooth boulder. But assuming it is an artificial object, we have to assume that Mars hosted orbital space traffic from a technological civilization in some previous era. That the civilization in question originated on Mars itself seems unlikely—Mars looks like it has been dry for long time, and the development of advanced lifeforms is assumed to need copious quantities of some kind of liquid medium.

But if you look in the mirror, you see a bipedal entity with grasping forelimbs and stereoscopic vision whose mastery of technology (as a species) has consumed only a twinkling of geologic time. The man-sized struthiomimus of the Late Cretaceous was also a bipedal entity with grasping forelimbs and stereoscopic vision. If some struthiomimus subspecies suddenly acquired some extra brain capacity and then achieved technological mastery (it's been demonstrated that the latter only takes a few centuries) there is no guarantee we would see evidence of it today, 65 million years later, especially if they favored wood construction and cremation burials.

The end of the Cretaceous period and the dinosaurs (including struthiomimus) apparently resulted from the Chicxulub meteor impact in what is now northern Yucatan. It is thought to have involved the impact of a celestial object approximately the size of Phobos.

Perhaps someone slipped up? Maneuvering those waystation asteroids could have been a tricky proposition. Perhaps they started out using the moon as a way station, and mined fuel there, but found that its 1/6-Earth gravity demanded too much additional fuel for takeoffs and landings. (We'll assume they were using chemical rockets similar to ours. Such rockets require about 25 pounds of fuel for every pound of payload lifted from the Earth's surface to Earth orbit. Getting into lunar orbit from the lunar surface takes about one pound of fuel for each pound of payload. Escaping Phobos's gravity would require a fuel-payload ratio equivalent to accelerating a truck once from zero to 25 miles per hour.)

Perhaps their success in putting low-orbit almost gravity-free yet mineable waystations in Martian orbit led them to try something similar in Earth orbit—unsuccessfully. Or perhaps they succeeded, but then went into decline due to the kind of internal conflict that is not unknown to humanity, leaving no one to perform orbital maintenance. (Phobos is expected to crash into Mars in several million years, and the results will not be pretty.)

Or maybe struthiomimus was just a chunky, prehistoric ostrich with grasping forelimbs (the name means "ostrich-mimic"), the monolith is just a boulder, and some obscure and currently unknown sequence of natural processes explains the presence and orbital characteristics of Phobos and Deimos.

But if they're not, we may end up accepting Phobos and Deimos as reverse anachronisms of the second kind, when in the future we figure out what they are and perhaps adopt similar space travel methods (hopefully without any Chicxulubs). With any luck the revelation will come gradually, giving us time to absorb the impact.

And that will give us plenty of time to ponder the fact that we somehow ended up naming the two surviving pieces of evidence Deimos and Phobos, Greek for Terror and Fear.

Conclusions

We've seen events described in detail before they took place, technologies in use before they were adopted or even discovered, knowledge that cannot be accounted for, behavior that implied foreknowledge, objects whose existence is inexplicable, and centuries-old artistic images that might as well have been made in Hollywood this morning.

What does it all mean?

The simplest answer is that the examples in this book again remind us that we don't understand the nature of time. Indeed, before we can complain that an example in this book violates the rules of time (as many seemingly do) first we have to define time—and that immediately gets us into trouble. According to the average dictionary, time is the interval between events. But what is the interval composed of? Time. So we are stuck in circular definitions.

Maybe time is just the fourth dimension, through which the other three must travel, undergoing some kind of cause-and-effect sorting as they do so. Or maybe it is a sort of infinite box containing all possible events, linked in a way that reflects someone's idea of cause-and-effect. We chose (probably collectively) to perceive selected events in a serial fashion, using some mechanism that maintains the linkages. Judging from the examples in this book, that mechanism may occasionally break down.

If we go ahead and accept the previous paragraph, it seems fair to say that human history can be viewed as a sort of ongoing experiment on the effects of the interaction of time (whatever it is) and the collective human consciousness. Perhaps human history can be compared to the particle accelerator experiments carried out by physicists, in which they examine the results of collisions between subatomic particles. The behavior of the particles after the collisions provides clues about the fundamental laws that govern the universe. In most cases, the collisions follow predictable patterns, but the outliers demand explanation—and the explanations often throw light on everything else.

The examples in the book can be considered outliers, the oddities that frame the norm. Meanwhile, human history is rich and long, and increasingly better documented. All indications are that the outliers gathered here are not even the tip of the iceberg, but just some snowflakes from its rim. Gathered in proper numbers and subjected to proper study, they could probably tell us a great deal about ourselves, and about time, and about how we and time mutually create each other—or about how time exists independently of us, and we are just hapless passengers aboard an onrushing train.

Alternately, we may confirm that we are simply not equipped to understand time. Our situation may be comparable to a computer, which does not know that its cover is painted blue, or understand the significance of those initials (IBM, we'll say) embossed there. It can be programmed to say that it knows, when asked. But the resulting answer is really just a linguist trick triggered by the programmer—the computer displays text, to which we assign meaning. Within the box itself there is no meaning or perception, only electrons being directed across transistors that are themselves under the control of other transistors, arranged in recurring patterns called logic gates.

But there is every indication that we need not fear what we discover, and that our expressions are not meaningless linguistic tricks triggered by an outside force. The sampling of human history contained in our examples shows that we are rarely content to follow the logic gates that are built into the circuitry. Rather, we feel compelled to make the logic gates serve us, to use them to launch explorations of the circuitry, until the components are mapped out, and we are pressing against the inside of the box.

Maybe someday we'll get to the outside. Maybe someday we'll even perceive the color of the cabinet, and read the embossed initials.

But we won't be able to do it without studying the outliers.

Bibliography

Access Hollywood. "Access Exclusive: Jennifer Aniston's Paparazzi Showdown in Mexico." 10 February 2010, *www.accesshollywood.com/access-exclusive-jennifer-anistons-paparazzi-showdown-in-mexico_article_28859.*

Adler, Jerry. "A 9,000-Year-Old Secret." *Newsweek,* 25 July, 2005, 52.

"Akhenaten." Last modified 3 May 2011, *http://en.wikipedia.org/wiki/Akhenaten.*

Andert, T.P., et al. "Precise Mass Determination and the Nature of Phobos." *Geophysical Research Letters* 37 (2010).

BBC News. "Ancient map with China at centre goes on show in US." 12 January 2010, *http://news.bbc.co.uk/2/hi/asia-pacific/8454049.stm.*

Bellamy, Edward. *Looking Backwards: 2000–1887.* On the Project Gutenberg Website. 2008 *www.gutenberg.org/files/624/624-h/624-h.htm.*

Beriwal, Madhu, and Avagene Moore. "Hurricane Pam and Hurricane Katrina." *Innovative Emergency Management, Inc.,* 14 December 2005. *www.emforum.org/vforum/lc051214.htm.*

BLAGO Fund, The. "Monastery Decani." http://www.srpskoblago.org/ Archives/Decani/exhibits/index.html.

Brucker, Joseph. "Matteo Ricci." *The Catholic Encyclopedia.* New York: Robert Appleton Company, 1911.

Bunch, Bryon H., and Alexander Hellemans. *The History of Science and Technology, A Browser's Guide to the Great Discoveries, Inventions, and the People Who Made Them From the Dawn of Time to Today.* Boston: Houghton Mifflin, 2004.

Bush, Vannevar. "As We May Think." *The Atlantic,* July 1945.

Bywater, Hector C. *The Great Pacific War: A History of the American-Japanese Campaign of 1931–33*. London: Constable and Co. Ltd., 1925.

Charles Babbage Institute, The. "Who Was Charles Babbage?" *www.cbi.umn.edu/about/babbage.html*.

Clarke, Arthur C. *2001: A Space Odyssey*. New York: New American Library, 1968.

CNN. "A Chronology: Key Moments in the Clinton-Lewinski Saga." *http://edition.cnn.com/ALLPOLITICS/1998/resources/lewinsky/timeline/*.

Cole, Hector. "Making Bradmore's Arrow Extractor." *www.evado.co.uk/Hector%20Cole/PDFs/BradmoreExtractor.pdf*.

Computer History Museum. "The Babbage Engine." *www.computerhistory.org/babbage*.

CSPAN. "Buzz Aldrin Reveals Existence of Monolith on Mars Moon." 22 July 2009, *www.youtube.com/watch?v=bDIXvpjnRws&eurl=http%3A%2F%2F*.

Cummins, Josephine. "Saving Prince Hal: Maxillo-Facial Surgery, 1403." *History of Dentistry Research Group, www.rcpsg.ac.uk/hdrg/2006Nov3.htm*.

Cuoghi, Diego. "The Art of Imagining UFOs." *The Skeptic* 11, no. 1 (2004) 43–51.

Custred, Glynn. "The Forbidden Discovery of Kennewick Man." *Academic Questions* 13, no. 3: 12–30.

Doug Engelbart Institute. "The Doug Engelbart Archives." *http://dougengelbart.org*.

Eckley, Grace. *Maiden Tribute: A Life of W.T. Stead*. Philadelphia: Xlibris Corp., 2007.

Engelbart, Doug. So-called "Mother of All Demos," 1968. *http://sloan.stanford.edu/MouseSite/1968Demo.html*.

European Space Agency. "Close Inspection of Phobos." *http://sci.esa.int/science-e/www/object/index.cfm?fobjectid=31031*. Accessed August 3, 2006.

Fanale, F.P. "Ice Distribution and Outgassing Rates for Ceres and Phobos: Theory vs. Observation." *Bulletin of the American Astronomical Society*, 22, p. 1122.

Faust, Drew Gilpin. "This Republic of Suffering: Death and the American Civil War." New York: Vintage Reprints, 2009.

Federal Emergency Management Agency, Baton Rouge. "Hurricane Pam Exercise Concludes." News release, 23 July 2004, *www.fema.gov/news/ newsrelease.fema?id=13051*.

Fischetti, Mark. "Drowning New Orleans." *Scientific American*, October 2001.

Fitzwilliam Museum, The. "Baptism of Christ." *www.fitzmuseum.cam.ac.uk/opac/ search/cataloguedetail.html?&priref=1418&_function_=xslt&_limit_=10*.

Freeth, Tony. "Decoding an Ancient Computer." *Scientific American*, December 2009, 76–83.

Friends of the Hunley. "History" sections. *www.hunley.org*.

Gibbs-Smith, Charles H. "Origins of the Helicopter." *The New Scientist*, 3 May 1962, 229–233.

Giuranna, M., et al. "Compositional Interpretation of PFS/MEx and TES/MGS Thermal Infrared Spectra of Phobos." *European Planetary Science Congress 2010*, *http://meetingorganizer.copernicus.org/EPSC2010/EPSC2010-211.pdf*.

GlobalSecurity.org. "Submarine History–The New Navy." *www.globalsecurity. org/military/systems/ship/sub-history4.htm*.

"Greek Temple." Last modified April 29, 2011, *http://en.wikipedia.org/wiki/ Greek_temple*.

Gregorie, Martin. "Flying the Saqqara Bird." *Catchpenny Mysteries*, 2002, *www.catchpenny.org/birdtest.html*.

Hadingham, Evan. "Unlocking the Secrets of the Parthenon." *Smithsonian Magazine*, February 2008.

Hall, James. *Dictionary of Subjects and Symbols in Art, Revised Edition*. New York: Harper & Row, 1979.

Hawass, Zahi. "King Tut's Family Secrets." *National Geographic*, September 2010.

Henkin, Hilary, and David Mamet. *Wag the Dog. New Line Cinema*, 1997.

"Iapetus (moon)." Last modified April 26, 2011, *http://en.wikipedia.org/wiki/Iapetus_(moon)*.

J. Paul Getty Museum, The. "Aert de Gelder." *www.getty.edu/art/gettyguide/artMakerDetails?maker=291&page=1*.

Kim, Eugene Eric, and Betty Alexander Toole. "Ada and the First Computer." *Scientific American*, May 1999, 76–81.

"Kosovo War." Last modified May 3, 2011, *http://en.wikipedia.org/wiki/Kosovo_War*.

Lanchester, F.W. *Aircraft in Warfare*. London: Constable and Co. Ltd., 1916.

Lanciani, Rofolpho. *The Ruins and Excavations of Ancient Rome*. New York: Houghton Mifflin, 1897. Excerpted at *http://aabbeatv.com/Pantheon/Pantheon.html*.

Lemonick, Michael D., and Andrea Dorfman. "Archaeology: The Amazing Vikings." *Time* May 8, 2000.

"Lewinsky Scandal." Last modified 26 April 2011, *http://en.wikipedia.org/wiki/Lewinsky_scandal*.

Linderman, Frank B. *American, The Life Story of a Great Indian*. New York: John Day Co., 1930. (Contains the dictated autobiography of Chief Plenty Coups.)

Lister, Joseph. "Antiseptic Principle of the Practice of Surgery." *Fordham University, www.fordham.edu/halsall/mod/1867lister.html*.

Livy. *History of Rome, Books IX to XXVI*. On the Project Gutenberg Website, 2004. *www.gutenberg.org/files/10907/10907-h/10907-h.htm*

Logan, Scott. "Viewing the Pup." *San Antonio Sky Watch*, January 7, 2010, *http://sanantonioskywatch.com/2010/01/17/viewing-the-pup/*.

Lovelace, Ada. "'Sketch of the Analytical Engine Invented by Charles Babbage,' by L. F. Menabrea with notes upon the Memoir by the translator Ada Augusta, Countess of Lovelace." *Scientific Memoirs, www.fourmilab.ch/babbage/sketch.html.*

Marysource.com. "Our Lady of the Snow." *www.marysource.com/apparitions/ourladysnow.htm.*

"Masolina de Panicale." Last modified January 7, 2011, *http://en.wikipedia.org/wiki/Masolino_da_Panicale.*

"Matteo Ricci." Last modified April 27, 2011, *http://en.wikipedia.org/wiki/Matteo_Ricci.*

Minnesota Public Radio. "Historic map coming to Minnesota." 16 December 2009, *http://minnesota.publicradio.org/display/web/2009/12/16/tulip-map.*

MIT, Course Announcements, Product Engineering Processes. "Archimedes Death Ray: Idea Feasibility Testing." October 2005, *http://web.mit.edu/2.009/www//experiments/deathray/10_ArchimedesResult.html.*

"Moons of Mars." Last modified April 27, 2011, *http://en.wikipedia.org/wiki/Moons_of_Mars.*

Moore, David. *The Roman Pantheon: The Triumph of Concrete. www.romanconcrete.com/.*

NASA. "Mars Global Surveyor, MOC Image 55103—Browse Page." *http://ida.wr.usgs.gov/html/orb_0551/55103.html* (eighth from top).

———. "Solar System Exploration." Iapetus page, *http://solarsystem.nasa.gov/planets/profile.cfm?Object=Sat_Iapetus.*

National Gallery, The. "The Annunciation, with Saint Emidius." *www.nationalgallery.org.uk/paintings/carlo-crivelli-the-annunciation-with-saint-emidius.*

Netz, Reviel, and William Noel. *The Archimedes Codex.* Philadelphia: Da Capo Press, 2007.

Ott, Michael. "Our Lady of the Snow." *The Catholic Encyclopedia.* New York: Robert Appleton Company, 1911.

"Pantheon." Last modified April 28, 2011, *http://en.wikipedia.org/wiki/Pantheon,_Rome*.

Plutarch. *Parallel Lives*. Project Gutenberg, 1996. *www.gutenberg.org/cache/epub/674/pg674.html*.

Polybius. *Histories*. New York: Macmillan, 1889. *www.perseus.tufts.edu/hopper/text?doc=Plb.+toc&redirect=true*

Reader, Colin. "Giza Before the Fourth Dynasty." *Journal of the Ancient Chronology Forum (JACF)* 9 (2002) 5–21, as reprinted at *www.thehallofmaat.com/modules.php?name=Articles&file=article&sid=93*.

Robida, Albert. *The Twentieth Century*. Middletown, Conn.: Wesleyan University Press, 2004.

Rugg, Gordon. "The Mystery of the Voynich Manuscript." *Scientific American*, June 2004.

"Sant'Emidio." *www.santemidio.com/*.

Science Museum, London. "Babbage." *www.sciencemuseum.org.uk/onlinestuff/stories/babbage.aspx*.

Suetonius. *The Lives of the Twelve Caesars*. Project Gutenberg, 2006. *www.gutenberg.org/files/6400/6400-h/6400-h.htm*.

Swift, Jonathan. *Gulliver's Travels*. Reprint of the 1892 version edited by David Price, Project Gutenberg, 2009. *www.gutenberg.org/files/829/829-h/829-h.htm*.

The Planetary Society. "Two-Faced Moon." *www.planetary.org/explore/topics/saturn/iapetus.html*.

"Mr. Charles Babbage (Obituary)." *The Times*, 23 October 1871.

Time. "Four Places Where the System Broke Down (in New Orleans During Katrina.)" 11 September 2005.

———. "Science: Bye, Columbus." 11 December 1978.

University Press. "The Parthenon." *www.ancientgreece.com/s/Parthenon/*.

Van Beek, Walter E.A., et al. "Dogon Restudied: A Field Evaluation of the Work of Marcel Griaule." *Current Anthropology* 32, no. 2, 139–167.

Verne, Jules. *From the Earth to the Moon* and *Round the Moon*. Project Gutenberg. *www.gutenberg.org/cache/epub/83/pg83.html*.

Vitruvius. *Ten Books on Architecture* (originally *De Architectura*). Project Gutenberg, 2006. *www.gutenberg.org/files/20239/20239-h/29239-h.htm*.

Voltaire. *Romans—Volume 3: Micromegas*. Translation by Peter Phalen, Project Gutenberg, 2009. *www.gutenberg.org/files/30123/30123-h/30123-h.htm*.

Wade, Mark. "Jules Verne Moon Gun." *Encyclopedia Astronautica, www. astronautix.com/lvs/julongun.htm*.

Wood, Lamont. "Forgotten PC History: The true origins of the personal computer." *Computerworld*, 8 August 2008.

———. History collection, Datapoint.

———. Notes, Doug Engelbart telephone interview, 20 September 1989.

Woodcroft, Bennett. *The Pneumatics by Hero of Alexandria*. London: Taylor Walton & Maberly, 1851, *www.history.rochester.edu/steam/hero/index.html*.

Index

About the Author

Residing in San Antonio, Texas, Lamont Wood has been a freelance writer since 1982, and has authored (or ghost-written) hundreds of magazine articles and nearly a dozen books. His work has appeared in publications ranging from the *Chicago Tribune* to *Scientific American* to *Computerworld* to trade journals in Hong Kong. Prior to that, he was a newspaper reporter and a publicity writer for a computer company. He is married to psychologist Louise O'Donnell, PhD, and has twin adult sons.

Searching For Answers...

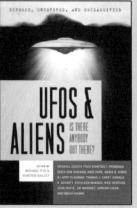
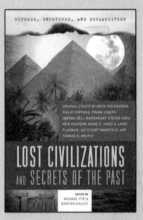
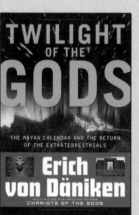